Early Start for Young Children with Autism/PDD

Practical Interventions

KATHLEEN McCONNELL

GAIL R. RYSER

Illustrations by Jenny Loehr

pro·ed
An International Publisher

8700 Shoal Creek Boulevard
Austin, Texas 78757-6897
800/897-3202   Fax 800/397-7633
www.proedinc.com

KH

© 2006 by PRO-ED, Inc.
8700 Shoal Creek Boulevard
Austin, Texas 78757-6897
800/897-3202   Fax 800/397-7633
www.proedinc.com

ISBN: 1-4164-0141-5

All rights reserved. No part of the material protected by this copyright notice may be reproduced or used in any form or by any means, electronic or mechanical, including photocopying, recording, or by any information storage and retrieval system, without prior written permission of the copyright owner.

NOTICE: PRO-ED grants permission to the user of this material to copy the appendixes for teaching purposes. Duplication of this material for commercial use is prohibited.

Illustrations by Jenny Loehr
www.curlygirlstudios.com

Printed in the United States of America

1   2   3   4   5   6   7   8   9   10   10   09   08   07   06

8/16/06

Contents

Introduction and Guidelines for Use

Early Start for Young Children with Autism/PDD: Practical Interventions was written to provide teachers, parents, interventionists, therapists, and caregivers with intervention strategies for young children with autism or another pervasive developmental disorder. While there are many materials written for school-age children with autism, very few educational products have focused specifically on young children, ages 2 through 5, with autism/PDD. This lack of materials is unfortunate, especially considering recent demographic trends related to the diagnosis of autism and the provision of services to children with the disorder. The rationale that follows discusses these trends in greater detail.

Rationale

In a 2001 study funded by the Office of Special Education Programs (OSEP), the National Research Council of the National Academies concluded that two key initiatives are critical to progress for children with autism: (a) early intervention and (b) a coordinated program of instructional strategies. The report to the National Institutes of Health (NIH) and the U. S. Department of Education emphasized that these initiatives are particularly important for young children with autism, a group whose numbers have increased recently and for whom programming remains a challenge. The policy paper recommended that children with autism be identified by age 2, but even before the NIH's recommendations were published, the number of infants and toddlers diagnosed as having autism was increasing. In 1976, the accepted prevalence rate for autism in early childhood was observed by Wing, Yeates, Brierley, and Gould in an epidemiological study completed in Camberwell, England. They found 5 cases in 10,000 children. Fombonne (2003) summarized the findings of 32 epidemiological surveys. He found that between 1966 and 1991 the rate remained at 4–5 per 10,000; but between 1992 and 2001, it increased to 12.7 per 10,000. As of December 1999, there were 205,352 infants and toddlers receiving early intervention services. More than one half of these children were ages 2 and 3. In addition, during the 1999–2000 school year, more than 65,000 students, ages 6 through 21, were served in the autism category of special education (Office or Special Education Programs, 2002). The autism category, established by the Individuals with Disabilities Education Act (IDEA) in 1997, is one of the fastest growing groups in special education.

Because a diagnosis of autism or a related disorder (including pervasive developmental disorder not otherwise specified, Asperger's disorder, Rett's disorder, or childhood disintegrative disorder) is based solely on behavioral criteria, intervention must address the child's behavioral needs. A study headed by Catherine Lord of the University of Chicago (Committee on Educational Interventions, 2001) recommended the following services as necessary for successful intervention:

- Intervention programs should begin as soon as the child is suspected of having an autism spectrum disorder.
- Intensive educational programming should take place for at least 25 hours a week, year-round.
- Programs should emphasize functional spontaneous communication.
- Social instruction should be delivered throughout the day in various settings.
- Programs should focus on cognitive development and play skills.
- Programs should take proactive approaches to behavior problems.

These instructional strategies are often recommended for young children but not always provided to them.

Early Start for Young Children with Autism/PDD is designed to meet the recommendations of the OSEP study. Specifically, many of the strategies presented in the book share the following important characteristics:

- They are techniques that can be implemented for children as young as 2 years.
- They can be used by teachers and parents as they seek to provide adequate hours of programming.
- They focus on communication.
- They incorporate social instruction into everyday situations.
- They incorporate play designed to increase cognitive development.
- They offer proactive approaches designed to teach good behavior.

We hope that you find the ideas presented here easy and practical to implement, especially for those of you who are parents or caregivers. Most suggestions can be tried at school or home with little or no equipment or prior training.

Our Characters

Intervention strategies should always fit your student's or child's personality and skill level. To help you match interventions with individual needs, we will use as examples three children of our own creation: Rusty, Caleb, and Lilly. Each child has a unique personality and interaction style, as well as an individual level of cognitive skills and behavioral competencies. While your own child or student may not exactly match any of our three children, you might be able to relate to one of them when we provide examples or suggest hypothetical situations. As you read, focus on the ideas that best meet your own child's needs.

Rusty is active and exuberant. He is constantly on the go and sometimes difficult to stop once he is focused on an activity. Rusty demonstrates some good skills in receptive language—he often understands what is said to him and follows some verbal directions. However, many of Rusty's behaviors are challenging for both his parents and his teachers.

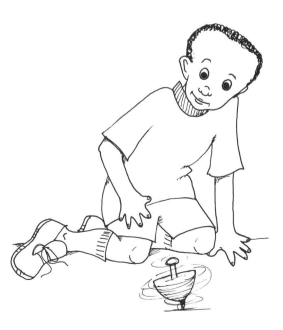

Caleb is often withdrawn into his own world. He often seems to look right though people and does not respond when his family or his teachers talk to him. Teaching Caleb basic skills requires a lot of repetition. While his behaviors are easier to manage than Rusty's, it can be difficult to keep him engaged and active. If the adults in Caleb's life do not push him to do things, he will sit and rock or engage in self-stimulatory behaviors like staring at the lights or flapping his hands.

⊙ **Lilly** often confounds the adults in her world. She repeats much of what is said to her and masters some skills quite easily yet has difficulty with some basics like turn taking and sharing. Lilly is more social than Rusty and Caleb but she does not engage in make-believe play or participate in activities with other children. Lilly has a loud, piercing squeal that she uses when she does not want to do something.

Rusty, Caleb, and Lilly have different strengths and challenges. They will appear throughout the book, and we hope that they make the content more relevant and enjoyable.

Components

In an effort to provide a comprehensive yet manageable amount of information, we have provided many references, sources of information, forms, and suggestions for related materials and products. While we do not endorse any specific products, we think it is helpful to guide our readers to related materials that they can review for themselves. Finally, in the Chapter 2 Appendix, readers will find a basic set of line drawings that can be used to construct materials like schedules, calendars, and so on.

As you read the book, we suggest you take notes, highlight, or mark specific information with note cards or tabs. This can help you as you design a specific plan for your young child with autism/PDD.

References

Committee on Educational Interventions for Children with Autism, Division of Behavioral and Social Sciences and Education, National Research Council. (2001). *Educating Children with Autism.* Washington, DC: National Academy Press.

Fombonne, E. (2003). Epidemiological surveys of autism and other pervasive developmental disorders: An update. *Journal of Autism and Developmental Disorders, 33*(4), 365–382.

Office of Special Education Programs. (2002). Twenty-Fourth Annual Report to Congress on the Implementation of the Individuals with Disabilities Education Act. Washington, DC: Author.

Wing, L., Yeates, S. R., Brierley, L. M., & Gould, J. (1976). The prevalence of early childhood autism: A comparison of administrative and epidemiological studies. *Psychological Medicine, 6,* 89–100.

CHAPTER

Create and Use a Visual Communication Framework

Autism is characterized by difficulties in three key areas: communication, socialization, and behavior. For young children with autism, the area of communication is particularly critical because their communication skills are just developing and may be significantly impacted by a developmental disability such as autism/PDD. For parents, caregivers, and teachers, maximizing the effectiveness of communication should be a primary focus.

While it is important to model, teach, and encourage young children with autism to speak, many of them will not develop meaningful spoken language at an early age. To communicate, these children must have some effective, efficient tools that allow them to exchange information, such as visuals. Instead of waiting to begin the teaching process until the child with autism is speaking, a teacher or parent can use visuals as communication devices, teaching tools, and a means for sharing information. In this chapter we will discuss the following visual communication strategies and supports for young children whose communication skills require them:

◎ Using basic principles as guidelines

◎ Using objects for communication

◎ Using visuals like photographs or icons

◎ Adding gestures and cues

◎ Organizing and storing visual cues

Guidelines

Use the following three research-based principles as a basis for your development and use of visual communication strategies with young children.

Use visuals that are portable and easily understood.

Visuals can go anywhere and represent almost anything. Using simple visual representations allows adults who work with young children with autism to communicate about almost anything, anywhere, at any time. Visuals should be portable, convenient, easily modified, and simple to understand. Many teaching systems, including the TEACCH (Treatment and Education of Autistic and other Communication handicapped CHildren) and PECS (Picture Exchange Communication System) programs, have promoted the use of visual tools for school-age children. In addition to using these highly respected and comprehensive programs, it is also important for teachers and parents to continue to use simple, basic visuals that meet children's needs as they arise. With an understanding of the flexible nature of visual communication systems, it is possible to prevent or respond to many different difficult situations as well as making teaching new skills easier and less stressful.

Use a communication format that fits the child.

There are several options for integrating visuals into your patterns of communication. These include the use of real-life objects, photographs, picture symbols, line drawings, or icons, and gestures or other physical cues. You can either use objects or use visual pictures or icons, which we refer to generally as visuals, but be consistent with your method. Either one is age appropriate and can be very effective for developing a system in which a young child can both understand and be understood.

Experiment with visuals.

The scope of using visuals with young children is unlimited. We will share many ideas with you for integrating visuals into your work with young children with autism, but we urge you to expand on the ideas presented. Don't be afraid to venture into uncharted visual territory. Keep in mind that visuals can augment almost any communication style or strategy, working side by side with other methods.

Objects

You may find that using objects is not necessary, because the child you are working with can understand photographs or drawings that are representative of real people, places, or things. However, because of their age and cognitive level, some children need real-life objects when first establishing patterns of communication. Using objects for communication may be less convenient that other modes of communication (less portable, less adaptable, more difficult to create), but the need to use objects to communicate may be only temporary. If you combine objects with more symbolic, less concrete visuals, as well as with words, young children will make the transition away from objects smoothly and quickly.

To begin to use objects in communication, start with the basic guidelines described below. This process will be easy for many parents and teachers because they are probably already doing many of the necessary steps without realizing it. Following are some ideas for establishing the relationship between objects and their meanings.

Consistently use one object to indicate one event, activity, person, or place.

If we want Caleb to get ready to sit on a carpet square on the floor, we will use two carpet squares that are alike in size, shape, and color. We put one carpet piece on the floor in Caleb's designated spot and give him the other. While

pointing to the carpet piece on the floor, we will direct Caleb to match his carpet square to the one on the floor, put it on top, and then "Sit." At first, we may have to assist him by helping carry the carpet, guiding him to the correct carpet square, or showing him how to sit. Gradually, we will reduce our prompts so that Caleb eventually does all the steps by himself. Our goal is that when Caleb is handed the carpet piece, he will walk to his spot, place the carpet piece on the floor, and sit down by himself. By using this object, the carpet square, we will have established meaningful communication. The carpet square will become associated with the word "sit." Its meaning should be clear and the need for prompting, coaxing, and repeated directions reduced.

Use a specific object to indicate transitions.

Using an object to signal a transition is an easy way to start establishing the meaning of an object. For example, if Lilly is having problems learning when to stop doing one activity and move to the next, we could hand her a small plastic clock and say, "Time to stop" whenever it's time to change. If we hand her the clock every single time we move from one task to the next, she should eventually learn that the clock means to end one thing and begin another. Transition objects can relate to the event they represent (e.g., fork means mealtime) or the concept of change (e.g., clock means time to change).

Create a tangible schedule with objects.

Introduce schedules into the educational plan for children with autism when they are young so that they learn to follow a sequence of activities and get into a predictable routine. Construct object schedules that are easy to use and easy for the child to understand. Begin by assembling a collection of small objects that represent activities. To arrange and present the objects, use one of the following simple formats.

Clear Plastic Hanging Shoe Storage Bag

Cut a horizontal or vertical strip of pockets off of the bag, or use one horizontal or one vertical line of pockets, and insert small objects into the sleeves. Each object will represent an activity, person, place, or thing. For example, a spoon can mean mealtime and a small metal toy car can mean that it's time to leave. Using the schedule is easy. Direct the child to each object when it is time to begin the activity. At first you may have to remove the object, walk the child to the activity location, and point out the next step. However, after several repetitions, adults should stand back and wait, using only gestures or cues to guide the child to the schedule and then the activity.

Plastic Box with Smaller Containers Inside

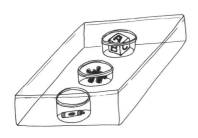

Another way to set up an object schedule is to buy a large, flat, clear plastic storage box. The box will represent the child's hour, morning, or day. Inside the flat box, arrange smaller plastic containers like tubs, food containers, or bowls. Keep the lids off. Place objects into the smaller containers in chronological order. The objects should be easy to manage without spilling or losing them. If the containers are too distracting for the child, just put Velcro strips on the inside bottom of the box and Velcro strips on the objects. Objects can then be directly attached to the box in

the right order. Again, teaching a young child to follow any schedule depends on repetition. We will discuss establishing and teaching routines in Chapter 5, but using common sense is always a good idea: The more consistently a routine is used, the more quickly it will be learned. Hand the child an object, move to the next activity, and repeat throughout the day.

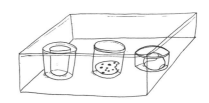

Tray with Velcro Squares Attached to the Surface

Begin by putting Velcro on the surface of the tray and the backs of the objects. Again, each object should stand for one specific action or activity and be used consistently to mean the same thing each time it is put on the schedule. For example, a toothbrush would indicate that it's time to brush teeth and a small washcloth would indicate bath time. Trays work well because they are portable. If you are teaching a young child in a preschool class to follow several different routines throughout the day, you can place objects on the tray to represent the steps of each routine. Getting off the bus, entering the school, walking to the classroom, putting a backpack on a hook, and sitting down can be the first routine. The next routine might involve going to the cafeteria, taking a tray, eating breakfast, wiping one's face, and throwing away trash.

The whole day can be structured with small objects, with each object representing an important activity for the child. Repeat until the child responds as soon as he or she is given an object.

Wooden Schedule Holder

Construct a holder that has a long piece of wood with dividers designed to resemble mail slots. Create three to five sections with the wood dividers but don't put a cover on them. This way, you can put objects into each section and the child can remove them easily. Each object is always visible to the young child. An example of a schedule that could be used with this format is shown below. It is Lilly's bath routine, indicated first by the rubber ducky (meaning bath

time), then by the washcloth and soap square (meaning she will have to use both in the tub), and finally by a small towel square (indicating that the last step is to be toweled dry). Because Lilly is sensitive to touch and often fights and screams when her mother tries to dry her off, letting Lilly know about the towel step is important.

Visuals

Visual representations of people, places, things, and actions can help the young child with autism understand others and can help the child initiate communication on his or her own. The visuals can be photographs, drawings, or picture symbols of the people and everyday items in the child's life.

Here are some examples of typical objects or actions that can be represented with simple line drawings, which are one of the most effective means of visual representation.

Toys, like a ball or doll

Pets, like a dog or cat

Objects, like a car or bed

People, like Mom or Dad

Actions, like brushing teeth or bathing

Introduce large, simple visuals.

If a child is young, you can make visuals meaningful in several ways. For example, you can use a large red stop sign that will be used as a signal to stop an activity. You can emphasize the visual even more if you laminate it and then put it on a tongue depressor or stick, so that you can hold it up easily and ensure its visibility, even when riding in a car or playing outside. Rusty, who is very active and exuberant, has problems stopping behaviors once he has started. Using a the stop sign along with a quick, firm verbal signal ("Stop") should help establish the concept for Rusty.

Using other generic visuals early with young children who have autism/PDD will enable you to integrate them later into instructional activities and behavioral systems. Generic visuals you should consider using include the following:

- The "no" symbol (a red circle with a diagonal slash through it)

- Red and green circles to represent "stop" and "go"

- Smiley faces: one turned up for happy and one turned down for sad

- A hand to represent waving hello and good-bye

Try different visual formats, and see which one works best.

If a child wants to spend all his or her time swinging, like Rusty does, either you can use a drawing of a swing to communicate or you can take a picture of the swing at the park where he or she likes to play. Try both visual styles and observe the reactions. If the child understands the photograph and responds to it more quickly than the drawing, then use the photo each time you communicate about swinging. Photographs are often effective because they are realistic and accurately represent objects or people, so you may find it more practical to use photos instead of drawings as you create a visual library. Because photographs are exact representations, young children might recognize and respond to them more easily than they would to symbolic representations. On the other hand, drawings are easy to find and use; there are many good sources of simple drawings in various sizes and with various levels of detail. At the end of this chapter, we have provided a collection of simple line drawings to help get you started.

Gestures, Physical Prompts, and Cues

Even though you are using visual representations like photographs, drawings, or picture symbols with young children, you will probably supplement these tools with physical prompts and cues. Most teachers and parents do this automatically and may not even realize how much they cue with eye gaze, facial expressions, body positions, and gestures. Because physical cues and prompts come naturally to most of us, they are easy to use and can be paired with the presentation of a visual. However, adults who work with young children who have autism should be careful to plan this pairing and make it purposeful.

There are several reasons to pair visuals with gestures. First, young children are often in settings or situations in which gestures or physical cues are more convenient and more universally understood. For example, when children are playing outside, gestures like waving and pointing are more visible and can be made more emphatic than visuals. Also, many parents would like their children to respond to more natural communication formats so that grandparents, neighbors, or caregivers can communicate effectively without a lot of extraneous materials. Finally, young children with autism can benefit from learning to "read" people's nonverbal signs. When taught to do so,

these children may fit in to some situations more easily than if they depend only on visuals.

Therefore, eventually, teachers or parents might want to phase out the constant use of visuals, especially when the child's spoken language improves. Remember, however, that the important point is for the child to understand and to be understood, so care should be taken not to remove visual supports that are still necessary.

Use consistent physical cues.

Consistency and predictability make learning easier. For example, if you want the child to check his or her schedule to see what's going to happen next, you could give the direction three ways:

① Point to the schedule.

② Say, "Time to check" or "Check schedule" (something short and direct).

③ Touch the first visual on the schedule.

If we consistently repeat this sequence with Rusty, he will soon learn to respond as soon as we point to the schedule and we won't have to chase him or lead him to the schedule. We can point and wait, then praise him when he responds.

Use the most common and practical gestures first.

Some physical movements are understood by almost everyone, regardless of age or cultural background. For example, pointing is a key gesture in communication and one that should be directly taught to a young child with autism if he or she is not using it. Pointing at something can enable the young child to indicate that he or she

- wants something

- sees something interesting

- recognizes someone or something familiar

- knows what another person is talking about (This is one way to teach and evaluate receptive language—asking the child to point at something and seeing if he or she is correct.)

Anytime you are using visuals with a young child, point clearly and directly at the visual with your index finger. Require the child to do the same if he or she is pointing to communicate with you. This is an important skill that should be demonstrated clearly and consistently. If Lilly gets to play with her doll after

completing a task in her preschool class, we will put the doll picture on her schedule so she knows that she has some playtime with it. We may also begin to require her to point at the doll on the shelf after removing the visual from her schedule. That way, we can be sure she knows that the picture of the doll represents the actual object—her real Raggedy Ann.

In the box that follows, we have provided a list of common gestures and physical movements that are typically used with preschoolers. Next to each gesture on the list is a simple drawing to show how you might represent the meaning of each. In addition, you may have other gestures unique to your classroom, family, or culture. Be ready to try any that you think the child will understand and use easily. Just don't overwhelm the child with too many gestures too quickly and be careful that each gesture is differentiated from others that might be similar. Otherwise, the child will be confused and communication will be difficult.

Gestures for Young Children

Hello and good-bye

Yes

Stop

Look

No

What?

Finished

Come here

More

Organization of Visuals

If you are going to use visuals effectively and efficiently, you will need to organize, maintain, and store them so that you can use them quickly and easily. To make your visuals practical for everyday use, consider formatting them so that they are sturdy and portable. If you are a teacher or other educator, laminate your visual materials so that they cannot be torn or crumpled. If you are a parent, try the following options:

① Ask a teacher or other service provider to laminate for you.

② Take your materials to an office supply store for coating.

③ Buy laminating sheets that are made to fit 8½″ × 11″ paper, or cover your visuals with wide bands of clear packaging tape.

It's always a good idea to make your materials so that they can be modified easily. One way to do this is to use Velcro or a similar fastener. That way, the schedule for the day can be easily changed as the people and events change. For example, Caleb's morning schedule usually includes eating breakfast, brushing his teeth, washing his face, and dressing. When his mother has an early day, however, she will sometimes have him eat breakfast at school, so she removes the "eat breakfast" visual from his schedule. It's not practical to create a brand-new schedule every time one part of it changes; just change, remove, or add the one part that is different.

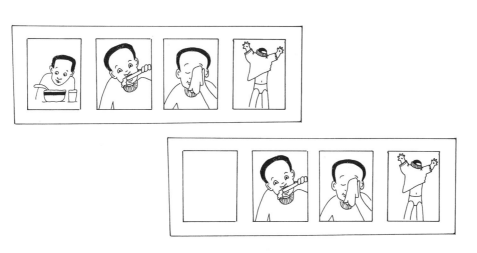

Use practical organization and storage systems.

There are many ways to store small or large visuals. Here are some of the most helpful ideas that we have seen.

Fishing Tackle Box

Plastic tackle boxes often have several pull-out drawers, tubs, and bins. They also have a lid that opens up to reveal additional storage sections that work well for storing small pictures and visuals. Organize your visuals in the drawers or sections alphabetically, by topic, by environment (home or school), or any other criteria that make sense in your situation. Before you purchase a tackle box, measure your visual cards to make sure they will fit into the storage sections.

Bulletin Board

Get an inexpensive bulletin board (or boards) and attach your visuals to it with pushpins or Velcro. To use Velcro, attach 1-inch Velcro squares or strips on the bulletin board surface and on the back of your visual cards. Arrange the visuals by category (people, places, things, etc.) so that they are visible and easy to locate. This method ensures that your visuals are easy to find, but it may not be practical for a large number of visuals. Therefore, this method should be reserved for your most frequently used pictures or symbols.

Photo Album or Notebook

Punch holes along the sides of heavy stock paper to make notebook pages. Then put 1-inch Velcro squares on the pages and attach your visuals to them. You can organize your visuals alphabetically or by category and add new notebooks or albums when needed. If you are a teacher, create two notebooks—one for school and one for home.

Plastic Bags

Put your visuals in clear, resealable plastic bags, then arrange the bags in a shoebox or file box. Because the bags are clear, you can easily see the visuals and find what you are looking for without a lot of trouble. If needed, attach letter tabs to the bags and arrange in alphabetical order for easier reference.

Supporting References and Resources

Bondy, A., & Frost, L. (2002). *A picture's worth: PECS and other visual communication strategies in autism.* Bethesda, MD: Woodbine House.

Keen, D., Sigafoos, J., & Woodyatt, G. (2001). Replacing prelinguistic behaviors with functional communication. *Journal of Autism and Developmental Disorders, 31*(4), 385–398.

Nigam, R. (2001). Dynamic assessment of graphic symbol combinations by children with autism. *Focus on Autism and Other Developmental Disabilities, 16*(3), 190–197.

Pierce, K., & Schreibman, L. (1994). Teaching daily living skills to children with autism in unsupervised settings through pictorial self-management. *Journal of Applied Behavior Analysis, 27,* 471–482.

Quill, K. (1997). Instructional considerations for young children with autism: The rationale for visually cued instruction. *Journal of Autism and Developmental Disorders, 27*(6), 697–714.

Schwartz, I., Garfinkle, A., & Bauer, J. (1998). The Picture Exchange Communication System: Communicative outcomes for young children with disabilities. *Topics in Early Childhood Special Education, 18,* 144–159.

Tissot, C., & Evans, R. (2003). Visual teaching strategies for children with autism. *Early Child Development and Care, 173*(4), 425–433.

Treatment and Education of Autistic and Related Communication Handicapped Children (TEACCH) is located in the School of Medicine at the University of North Carolina at Chapel Hill. It was founded by Dr. Eric Schopler and began as a federally funded research project in the early 1970s. To find out more about Division TEACCH see www.teacch.com.

CHAPTER 2 APPENDIX

Reproducible Line Drawings

Note. The line drawings in this appendix are from *Teaching Kids & Adults with Autism: Building the Framework for Lifetime Learning* (pp. 287–301), by K. McConnell Fad and R. Moulton, 1999, Longmont, CO: Sopris West. Copyright 1999 by K. McConnell Fad and R. Moulton. Reprinted with permission of the authors and the publisher.

alphabet

apple

baby

backpack

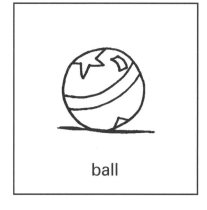

ball

banana

bath

bathroom

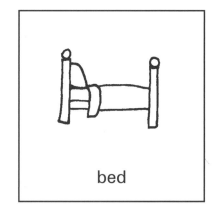

bed

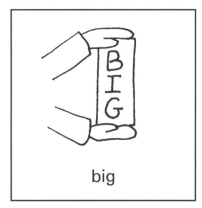

big

book

breakfast

24

brush

bus

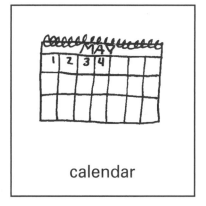

calendar

car

cartoons

cat

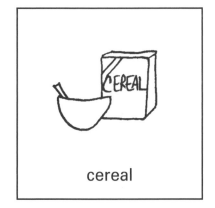

cereal

cheese

chicken nuggets

church

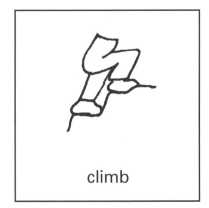

climb

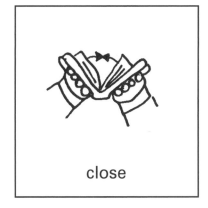

close

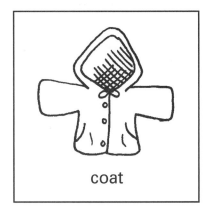

coat

cold

color

come

computer

cry

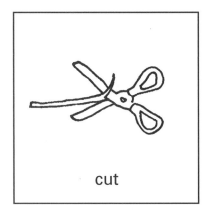

cut

dinner

dog

doll

door

draw

drink

eat

excited

french fries

fruit

frustrated

funny

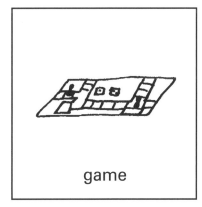

game

grocery store

happy

hi

hot

hungry

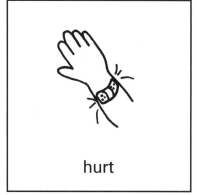

hurt

juice

kick

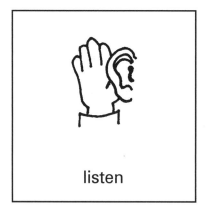

listen

lunch

milk

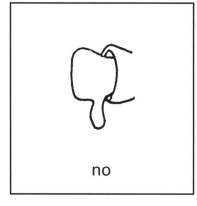

no

open

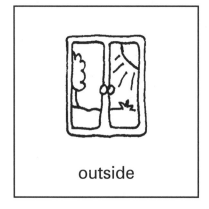

outside

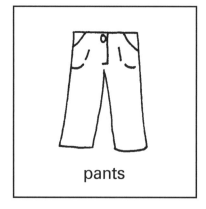

pants

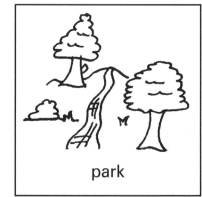

park

pencil

pizza

play

playground

puzzle

quiet

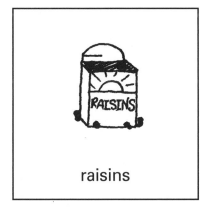

raisins

read

recess

run

sad

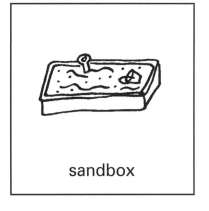

sandbox

sandwich

scared

school

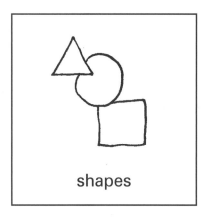

shapes

share

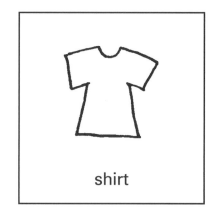

shirt

shoes

shorts

sing

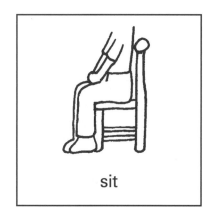

sit

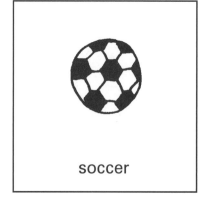

soccer

socks

stop

store

swimming pool

swing

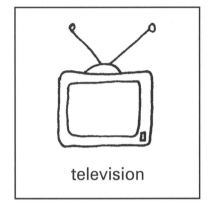

television

throw

time

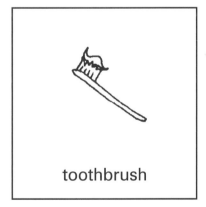

toothbrush

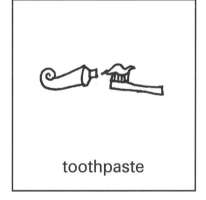

toothpaste

toy

tricycle

truck

underwear

upset

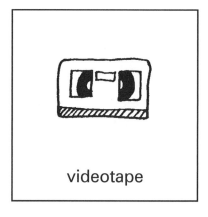

videotape

wagon

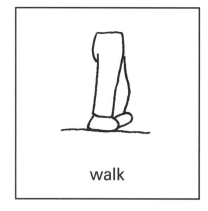

walk

wash

water

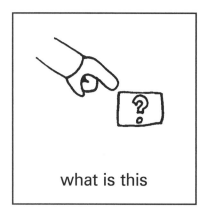

what is this

where is . . .

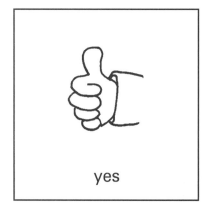

yes

yogurt

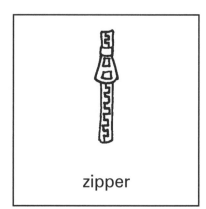

zipper

3

Structure the Environment

After establishing effective communication strategies with the young child who has autism/PDD, teachers and parents can shift their focus to structuring the child's environment. This chapter provides the following strategies:

◉ Using guidelines for structuring the environment

◉ Organizing and labeling objects in the child's environment

◉ Structuring the learning environment

The same visuals that are used for daily communication can be used to promote independence. This shift toward independent functioning is more likely if the environment is structured so that the preschooler can do more with less adult direction. For example, when Caleb is at home, he will be more likely to do the following if visuals are well integrated into his environment:

◉ Find his own toys if his toy box is labeled with pictures of the items inside

◉ Follow the necessary steps in brushing his teeth if he has a picture schedule that shows him how to do it

◉ Gather his backpack and lunch box on the way out the door if he has a picture cue reminding him to do so

Similarly, at school, Lilly can do the following:

- Point to what she wants to eat when provided a picture menu.

- Sit in her assigned spot if her picture and name are used to label it.

- Remember to wash her hands after using the bathroom when she sees the cue on the bathroom door.

Guidelines

The level of organization applied to a classroom or home environment should depend on the needs of the child. Generally, the more structure, the better for young children with autism. Young children with autism/PDD often have limited communication skills, difficulties with transitions, and a tendency to become passive if they are not kept involved in productive activities. There are many organizational strategies that can be used with young children who have autism. The ideas that follow are helpful when structuring any environment for a young child with autism/PDD.

Place visual cues at the child's eye level.

Remember that you are teaching a young, small child. When integrating visuals into the child's environment, place them at the child's eye level and in clearly visible places. For example, if Lilly likes to run out of the classroom and refuses to stop when told, a stop sign placed by the door is a good visual reminder. She needs to see the sign in order to respond, so we place it below the doorknob, at her eye level.

Use the same visual tools in all environments.

If you are a teacher in a preschool program for children with disabilities or an interventionist or therapist in an early childhood program, you can help ensure consistency by making duplicate or even triplicate sets of any visuals that you use with a child. Share the visuals with families and caregivers. Likewise, if you are a parent and have found some specific visual tools that are working well with your child, share them with the professionals and others in your child's life. If a young child with autism or another PDD goes to a private preschool, play group, babysitter, or family member caregiver, each of those environments should be

using the same system of communication. The child will learn much more quickly if communication is consistent across environments. For example, if Rusty's visual reminder card cueing him to stay with the adult supervising him (instead of running away) is used by everyone, he may be more likely to stay with his mother in the grocery store, remain in the preschool classroom, and hold his grandmother's hand when she takes him for a walk.

Make visuals portable.

One way to promote consistency of communication is to use tools that can work easily in all environments. Because much of the instruction for preschoolers is designed to be active, communication tools should be portable and flexible. It is developmentally appropriate for young children to be constantly on the go and preschoolers typically don't sit still or work at desks or tables for long periods of time. In addition, much of the instruction in programs designed to meet their

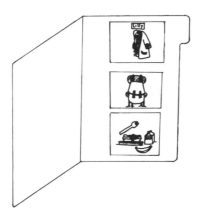

needs is focused on play-based activities. Communication systems, therefore, should be responsive to these instructional issues and may not be the same as communication systems designed for older children. Consequently, if you are going to use a schedule, for example, put it inside a folder, on a small strip of stiff poster or project board, in a small photo album, or on a key ring so it can go anywhere.

Make sure everyone uses the same visual cues.

Using visual cues consistently helps children generalize learned skills to all environments and people. For example, Caleb's preschool teacher and Caleb's parents both use a small folder that includes photos that show how Caleb is supposed to sit while riding in a car or on the bus. Because Caleb is belted into a car seat when he travels on the school bus and belted into a car seat in the family car, the picture will have meaning for him in either situation. He also has the same rules in both situations: "Stay buckled" and "No screaming."

When Caleb gets in the car in the morning, the sign is attached with Velcro to the back of the seat in front of him. When he gets on the

school bus in the afternoon, the sign goes with him again and is attached with Velcro to the back of the seat in front of him. Because the sign is lightweight and simple, it can be used conveniently everywhere.

Objects in the Environment

Now that some general guidelines have been provided, we will suggest methods of organizing the environments of young children with autism or PDD. First, a decision should be made both in the preschool or day care and the home about which items will be accessible to the child. Accessibility will depend in part on the purpose of the items.

For example, if you are teaching Caleb to choose one of two toys to play with and you want him to make the choice independently, you will want to make both toys accessible. This means placing them low enough to reach and in an unobstructed location like an open shelf or on a table. The place where each toy is stored should have a visual attached to it, either a photograph, a line drawing, or an icon, depending on the child's style of communication.

For Caleb, we use a photograph or line drawing because an icon is too abstract for him. The visual label is important because when Caleb is finished playing with the toy, his teacher wants him to return it to its place. If the toy is in the same place each time Caleb goes to get it, he will quickly learn how to find it easily. This predictability should help reduce his frustration and increase his independence. On the other hand, if items are off-limits due to a safety hazard or other reason, place them out of reach in an inconspicuous location.

Organize and label toys.

Toys are the teaching tools for preschoolers. They can be organized in several effective ways, including the following.

Cubbyholes or Open Shelves

Cubbies and shelves are often standard in preschool classrooms. Cubbies are great because they don't have a front piece that obstructs the child's view and they don't have a door that is difficult for a young child to open. When using cubbies for storage, make sure to place a piece of Velcro to the front or top of the cubby or shelf so that you can attach a visual label. The picture label will  help the child remember what is contained in the space and prompt him or her to return it to its proper place.

Plastic Tubs

Plastic tubs come in many different sizes and shapes. They work well for toys because they hold lots of items, especially small toys, and they are spill-proof when the lids are on tight. Tubs should be clear so that the child can see the toys inside. Also, put visual labels on the lid or front panel of each tub to help the child know which tub holds which toys. During those times when you want the child to have unlimited access to toys in the tubs, make sure you partially or totally remove the lids, so he or she is not frustrated by a difficult-to-open container.

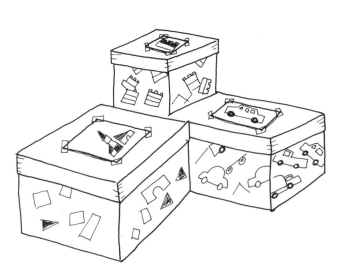

Racks with Open Tubs

Several discount department stores sell children's storage units, many with open plastic bins that slide over bars and rest at a downward angle. These storage units can help preschoolers get organized. The colored bins are especially helpful for children with autism who may learn where things go more quickly if items are sorted and stored based on the color of the bin.

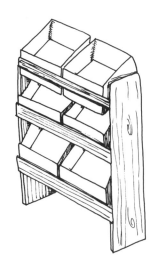

Laundry Baskets, Waste Baskets, and Playpens

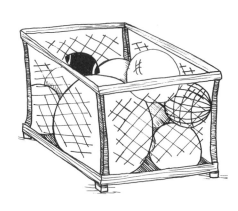

It is always helpful to have some large toys available for young children with autism. They work well for turn-taking activities and for children who need to improve their gross-motor skills. Toys like beach balls, bouncing balls, and exercise mats can be used for gross-motor activities. Such large toys will need to be stored in large containers like laundry baskets and even playpens. You may find it helpful to label these large containers with pictures of what is inside.

Plastic Buckets and Tubs

Small plastic buckets also function well for many young children with autism who have sensory preferences. These children like to sift dried rice or beans in tubs, swish their hands in buckets of water, or squeeze squishy mixtures like clay or playdough. Of course, you won't allow a child to have access to small objects unless you are closely supervising and are sure that the child does not put them in his or her mouth.

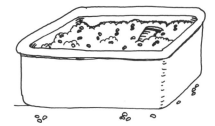

Small Wading Pools

If you have the space in your classroom or home, small wading pools are great play areas for preschoolers with autism. The pools provide boundaries for the

children and can hold small toys, be filled with sand to make a sandbox, and, of course, be filled with water during warm weather. Be sure to label the pool and, if you have more than one, make sure the picture represents what is inside the pool, not just what it looks like outside.

Organize clothes and personal items.

Many of the skills that young children need to learn are related to dressing and self-care. While it is not likely that a preschool-age child will be totally independent in caring for himself or herself either at school or home, a structured, organized environment will make it much easier to teach necessary skills. Here are some tools for organizing clothing and other personal care items for young children.

Hooks and Racks

Many young children who have difficulty with motor tasks or complicated systems of storage will have trouble accessing clothing stored on hangers in a closet or folded in dresser drawers. To increase their independence in dressing or managing their clothing, backpacks, hats, or shoes, young children with autism/PDD should have simple storage systems. Large hooks and open racks that a young child can reach easily will encourage independence. For Rusty, we have a large hook with a picture of his jacket posted on the wall below it. He can put his jacket on the hook when he gets to school, and then easily retrieve it by himself when it's time to play outside. The adults in his preschool classroom will encourage him to do both things independently.

Bins and Cubbyholes

We often think of plastic storage bins and cubbyhole shelves for toys, books, and other learning tools, but we forget about using them for children's personal items. Bins can be used for clothing, school supplies, or special items such as "blankies."

Metal Storage Systems

Open-grid metal storage systems that have adjustable shelves and drawers also work well for storage. Children can see the items inside each drawer and easily slide them out. When adults are teaching children to be more independent, this type of storage can be helpful at both home and school. Of course, when you want to keep certain items out of sight, you will need to find a high shelf, drawer, cabinet, or even the trunk of your car for storage.

Learning Environment

Whether you are organizing a preschool classroom or a home where you will be teaching a young child with autism/PDD, it is important to structure the overall environment, not just the items in it. Many preschool teachers have had little education and training specific to autism or little experience with children who have autism. These teachers, whose classes more commonly include children with less pervasive or complicated disabilities, may find the level of structure needed for children with autism overwhelming. Parents, too, may find it difficult to establish and maintain structure and consistency in their child's home environment, especially if the child with autism has brothers and sisters. Such structure, however, is integral to the success of a child with autism. The following sections explain how to arrange the classroom and establish clear boundaries to maximize learning.

Arrange the classroom.

Establishing an effective learning environment for preschool children with autism/PDD requires clear physical and visual boundaries. The preschool classroom for children with autism/PDD should include areas for several different types of instructional activities. Ideally these would include the following.

Small Play Areas

A key problem for children with autism is failure to engage in make-believe play. Play provides a perfect environment for teaching language, social, and behavioral skills for young children. Provide areas that can accommodate one or more students for specific types of play. A block center, small play kitchen, listening center, reading area, work table for clay or playdough, music and dance area, art area with easels, and puppet or doll area can all be used during play time. Specific skills can be encouraged and modeled in the play areas. For example, if we want Lilly to work on listening, we will make sure that she has plenty of time set aside in the listening center to listen to music on tapes.

Quiet Space

Young children who are active need rest throughout the day. Because children with autism may have sleep problems, it is important to design an environment that allows for rest and calm time, even if sleep is impossible. Establish a quiet space for use during rest times. Floor mats, carpet sections, or air mattresses can be used in preschool settings or at home.

One-to-One Instructional Areas

There should be at least a couple of one-to-one areas in a preschool classroom that includes children with autism. Because these classes typically have a small number of students, the areas can be used by individual students on a rotating basis. One-to-one instructional areas may include a carpet area that is bordered

with tape or paint, a small table with chairs opposite or next to each other, or just a small chair for the child. Allocating floor space for instruction is important for preschool children, because sitting at a desk for extended periods is tiring and is not the best setting in which to teach some skills.

Independent Work and Play Areas

As preschool children mature and develop more independence, they should be able to work and play with less support. Setting up a desk or floor area with a physical buffer like a bookshelf or room divider is helpful as children learn to work alone and attend to tasks without constant cues or prompts. Visual supervision should always be maintained, however, and the work area should never be designed to seclude a child.

Large Areas

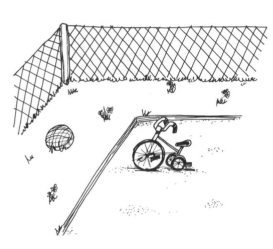

Whether the young child with autism is receiving physical or occupational therapy, space should be available to run, throw balls, ride a scooter or tricycle, swing, or engage in other large-muscle activities. Provide areas both outdoors and indoors for play and motor skills education. Many important skills are taught through structured play activities and attention should be paid to this area of development.

Bathroom and Changing Area

Many young children with autism/PDD will begin preschool before they have been fully potty trained. To facilitate the teaching of this important skill and to maintain children's privacy, the preschool classroom should have a screened, private area for changing diapers or clothes. While classrooms in newer buildings often have these areas built in during construction, older rooms may require curtains attached to the ceiling, portable folding screens, or room dividers. Padded tables can be purchased from companies that sell adaptive equipment.

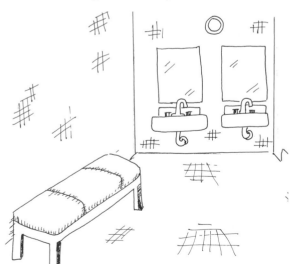

Sink and Counter Area

Self-care skills are critical for young children with autism. Turning a faucet on and off, washing and drying hands, getting a drink independently, and cleaning up a play or work area are all good skills to teach the preschool child with autism. The instruction should occur often throughout the day, at normal times and in typical situations. Trying to teach skills in isolation and then generalize them to everyday situations is not nearly as efficient. Many preschool classrooms are built with counter space and sinks, which are needed often during the school day.

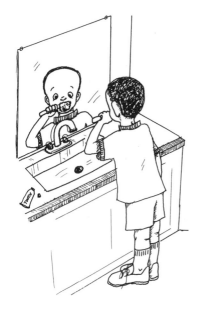

Optional Areas

The areas mentioned above can easily be supplemented with other classroom spaces. For example, some preschool classrooms for children with disabilities include outdoor water areas or gardens. Others include computer instruction sections. While budgets and space may determine the full extent of the preschool environment, learning areas should be designed to teach the child with autism in each of the disability areas: communication, socialization, and behavior.

For parents and caregivers, most of the areas described in the preceding section are already present in the home. The challenge is to clearly delineate them so that your child understands the boundaries of each. Differentiating areas by purpose, labeling them, and using each area for a specific purpose will help teach the child what to do and where to do it.

Create boundaries.

Once you have decided on the areas you want in the learning environment, they must be clearly identified. This can be done several ways.

Furniture

One of the easiest and most effective methods of dividing a classroom or other large area into small sections is to use furniture. Large, solid pieces like bookcases, shelving units, or filing cabinets are often available. These dividers are great because they also serve a second function, storage. Each piece of furniture should be double-checked to ensure that it is stable and untippable. Furniture establishes clear boundaries and minimizes visual distractions from other parts of the room.

Portable Boundaries

Classrooms and home spaces can also be divided by portable dividers like folding room dividers, office panels, or racks that hold charts or write-on boards. These dividers work well because they can easily be moved, allowing for flexibility in work space. Again, caution should be used when setting up portable dividers because they may fall or tip easily.

Line Boundaries

Having lots of small spaces in a classroom or home is often impractical and may even be a bad idea for young children who have problems working in confined spaces. Line boundaries can be used to designate a specific space without closing in the area. To make line boundaries on the floor, use colored duct tape or electrical tape. Colored masking tape works well to divide the space on walls or bulletin boards. Separating sections of the room with large blocks of color, like different colors of rugs or mats, also helps young children understand boundaries.

Covers and Curtains

Some areas of a classroom or home may be off-limits to young children part of the day and accessible part of the day. Young children with autism may have difficulty understanding this change so it will help to put drapes or covers over particular shelves, toys, racks, or objects when the adults decide that the items are not appropriate for use. It is often a lot easier to remove things from sight than fight a battle over their use. Large pieces of fabric like sheets, curtains, or drapes are easy to use and store for adjusting the child's environment.

Distractions and Visual Clutter

Many young children with autism have difficulty functioning in busy, cluttered environments. These children may not be able to focus on assigned tasks and may become overstimulated and confused if there is too much going on at once. Store objects out of sight and do not display an excess of bright visuals, signs, posters, or stacks of materials.

Supporting References and Resources

Dahle, K. B. (2003). Services to include young children with autism in the general classroom. *Early Childhood Education Journal, 31*(1), 65–70.

Heflin, L. J., & Alberto, P. A. (2001). Establishing a behavioral context for learning for students with autism. *Focus on Autism and Other Developmental Disabilities, 16*(2), 93–101.

Marcus, L., Schopler, E., & Lord, C. (2000). TEACCH services for preschool children. In J. S. Handleman & S. L. Harris (Eds.), *Preschool Education Programs for Children with Autism* (2nd ed., pp. 215–232). Austin, TX: PRO-ED.

McGee, G. G., Daly, T., Izeman, S. G., Man, L., & Risley, T. R. (1991). Use of classroom materials to promote preschool engagement. *Teaching Exceptional Children, 23,* 44–47.

Rogers, S. J., & Lewis, H. (1988). An effective day treatment model for young children with pervasive developmental disorders. *Journal of the American Academy of Child and Adolescent Psychiatry, 28,* 207–214.

Schwartz, I. S., Sandall, S. R., McBride, B. J., & Boulware, G. L. (2004). Project DATA (developmentally appropriate treatment for autism): An inclusive school-based approach to educating young children with autism. *Topics in Early Childhood Special Education, 24*(3), 156–168.

Simpson, R. L., & Myles, B. S. (1998). Understanding and responding to the needs of students with autism. In R. L. Simpson & B. S. Myles (Eds.), *Educating children and youth with autism: Strategies for effective practice* (pp. 1–23). Austin, TX: PRO-ED.

Develop Schedules and Calendars

Structuring the physical environment, as discussed in the last chapter, is the first step toward getting organized when working with very young children who have autism/PDD. A second important component of environmental organization is structuring how adults and children use their time. This chapter provides the following information:

◉ Using guidelines to develop schedules and calendars

◉ Developing schedules for adults

◉ Developing schedules for children

◉ Creating calendars

Without attention to time management, many children with autism/PDD will experience difficulties in transitions, changes, and adaptations to routines. Sometimes these difficulties are minor, as when Caleb cries if his teacher, Mrs. Lane, does not greet him as he gets off the bus.

Problems caused by a lack of structure can also be more serious, however, such as Rusty having a tantrum if he has to work one-to-one with his teacher while other students are in the block center of the room. Using a schedule with Rusty will help him understand that after he finishes his work, it will be his turn to play.

Not every behavior problem or difficulty is due to the amount or quality of organization in an environment and not every behavior problem can be avoided by attending to environmental issues. However, prevention is always the first approach to try when addressing behavioral issues. Tools like schedules, calendars, and communication systems are positive supports for both children and adults.

Guidelines

Young children with autism/PDD function better in organized environments because of their communication problems, behavior issues, and lack of social interaction skills. Unpredictable, chaotic situations can cause anxiety and panic. It is also easier to learn when there is predictability in the presentation of content and in required responses. Here are some key points to remember as you increase the level of organization in your classroom or home. These guidelines will help you develop effective schedules and calendars.

Make schedules accessible.

Schedules should always be posted so that anyone entering the room knows exactly who is doing what with whom. This is especially true in situations where there are several different service providers in addition to teachers and instructional assistants. Many young children with autism have speech, occupational, physical, or music therapy or adaptive physical education, as well as services from behavior specialists or psychologists. When schedules are not easy to find, planning and communication are difficult.

Keep it simple.

Parents and teachers of children with autism/PDD are usually very busy. Any type of organizational scheme must be designed to save time not take time. Color coding, visual cues, easy-to-read font type, and consistent format communicate information more effectively than haphazard or random systems.

Use schedules and calendars as teaching tools.

Long-term calendars or complicated schedules are not likely to be understood by young children with autism/PDD. However, if young children are introduced to simple schedules and calendars and taught to use them, as they get older they will be able to understand more complex, long-term systems. Schedules can be used to teach communication skills, key behaviors like following directions, and social skills like turn taking and waiting.

Adult Schedules

The typical early childhood class, prekindergarten class, or day-care center is a busy place. There are often many children and several adults in these environments. Unfortunately, the presence of more people in the environment does not always result in better use of time or a more productive setting. To ensure maximum efficiency, schedules should be created for the adults in the classroom. Each adult should know exactly what he or she is supposed to do at any given moment of the day. There are several good reasons to create, post, and follow a schedule when working with very young children who have autism or other developmental disabilities. A schedule keeps busy adults in tune with what should be happening. There are always unexpected events or minor crises, but teachers and instructional assistants need to maximize the time their students spend on task. Educational research about time on task is thorough and demonstrates obvious conclusions: The more time students are on task (i.e., focused on learning), the more they learn. The following are some simple, clear strategies for establishing and maintaining schedules for adults.

Use a linear timeline.

Morning Lesson Plans

Teacher's Name Stan Rivera   Date March 1–April 2

	Monday	Tuesday	Wednesday	Thursday	Friday
8:00	greeting & breakfast				→
8:30	circle time				→
9:00	centers	Rusty speech	centers	centers	centers
9:30	individual activities	Caleb speech	individual activities	Lilly speech	individual activities
10:00	snack & read aloud				→
10:30	music	P. E.	recess	P. E.	art
11:00	hands-on learning				→
11:30	lunch				→

Most of us follow a work schedule that is relatively consistent from day to day. In a busy classroom, it is helpful to develop a simple timeline of activities for the day. Many of the learning activities for very young children who have disabilities are designed to include play, music, art, reading aloud, and hands-on activities. Young children with autism/PDD, like all children their age, need some "down time," but the classroom should have a high commitment to teaching and learning while students are present.

The example shown is a morning schedule for adults, shown in a vertical time-line. Next to each time is an activity typical of a preschool class that includes children with autism/PDD. This schedule is not the only organizational tool, but rather the first building block for a well-organized learning environment. We have provided several blank forms in Appendix 4 (pp. 60–62) that can be used to design this type of schedule.

Parents and caregivers can use this format for after-school and weekend schedules for children. List times in increments of 15 to 30 minutes and then write down specific activities next to each time period. If this type of schedule is written on a large whiteboard and posted in a central location like the kitchen, everyone can keep track of activities and make sure that goals are accomplished.

Use a block chart.

The example that follows shows a simple block chart designed to function as a daily morning schedule. This schedule explains the activities of therapists, the teacher, and the assistant as the day progresses from drop-off time at 7:45 until lunch time at 11:45. On the schedule, you can see in the left-hand column the list of therapists and the times that they will be working with students. Because autism is a pervasive disability that impacts so many areas of development, most young children who have autism/PDD receive several different types of service, including speech–language therapy, occupational therapy, and physical therapy. In the example, you can see that those individuals are shown, along with the times and days of the week that they are assigned to work with students. The middle column is the teacher's schedule. The times correspond to those in the left column and at each time period listed, it is easy to see what the teacher is doing and which students are assigned to him. The right side of the schedule details the duties of the instructional

Our Morning Schedule

Time	Related Services	Teacher Stan	Aide/Para. Michelle
7:45		greet children	meet children at bus
8:00		lead group in morning routine	take attendance to office
8:15		circle time	assist with circle time
8:30		whole–group language lesson	assist with whole–group language lesson
8:45	M W F OT: Lilly	small group	individual work with Caleb
9:00	M W F Speech: Caleb	small group	small group
9:15		individual work with Rusty	small group
9:30	T Th OT: Rusty	snack and restroom	snack and restroom
9:45	Th PT: Lilly		adaptive P. E.
10:00		individual work with Lilly	adaptive P. E.
10:15	T Th OT: Caleb	whole group	
10:30	M W F Speech: Rusty	center rotation	assist with center rotation
10:45		center rotation	assist with center rotation
11:00	T Th Speech: Lily	center rotation	assist with center rotation
11:15		whole–group social skills development	story time
11:30		lunch	lunch
11:45			

assistant. As you can see, some of the assistant's responsibilities are shared with the teacher and others are designed to provide support to specific students.

One advantage of this schedule format is that it is simple and easy to understand. Professionals who want to use this type of schedule can create a template as a computer file so that the basic schedule is always available. The schedule can easily be changed to accommodate personnel or time changes or to vary assignments as students enter or leave the program. You can find blank versions of block chart schedules in Appendix 4 (pp. 63–64).

Whether you use the linear timeline or the block chart, you should enlarge your schedule and post it in the classroom. That way, anyone who enters the room can immediately determine what everyone should be doing. Posting the schedule also helps staff members remain focused on the time periods and what is to be accomplished during those time periods. While some flexibility is always necessary in any classroom, students will learn more if adults remain focused on accomplishing established goals.

Organize charts by individual students or groups.

When a student's educational program is highly individualized or when there are very few students in the classroom, it may be more practical to create a schedule by student rather than by adult. We have provided an example of this type of schedule format below. One advantage of a student-based schedule is that it can be linked directly to the student's Individualized Education Program (IEP). The daily schedule will show that each required service, instructional arrangement, or activity is provided. Two blank forms are provided in Appendix 4 (pp. 65–66).

Daily Schedule

Time	Group 1 Lilly, Randy	Group 2 Caleb	Group 3 Rusty, Jimmy
7:45	breakfast	arrive	arrive
8:00	circle time	circle time	circle time
8:30	language lesson	speech	speech
9:00	speech	OT	PT
9:30	center 1	center 2	center 3

Student Schedules

Chapters 2 and 3 provided information about the use of visuals with young children who have autism/PDD. Once the use of visuals has been established, teachers and parents can begin to teach young children with autism to follow simple schedules that include one or two activities. As the children mature, additional activities can be added. There are several strategies for creating student schedules, whether they are used at home or at school.

Match colors or shapes to locations or activities.

Young children, especially those with communication delays, can be directed to activities, people, or places by using colors or shapes. For example, a teacher could hang a large red circle over the one-to-one learning area. If Lilly is scheduled to work in this area, she will be handed a smaller red circle and guided to the one-to-one area by the teacher. Once there, the teacher will hold up her circle to the other, repeat "red circle, Lilly," and then seat her at the desk or table, which also has a red circle taped to it. By repeating this routine daily or several times each day, hopefully with less and less guidance, Lilly should one day be handed the red circle and immediately walk to her assigned area.

Expand the schedule with a pocket chart.

While parents may not be familiar with pocket charts, most preschool and elementary school teachers use these tools for instruction and organization. These charts are usually made of durable, stiff plastic and include rows of small pockets that have clear plastic fronts, so that anything placed in the pocket is visible. While they are often used to hold numbers and letters, pocket charts can be a great first schedule for very young children with autism/PDD.

To create a pocket-chart schedule, start with a small chart with 4" × 4" squares. The chart can be hung from a chart holder or attached to a bulletin board or wall. When using the pocket chart with very young children, it is important to place it at their eye level. Photos of the children, labeled with their names, should be placed in the first column, down the left side of the chart. Each child's activities will be determined by the squares placed in his or her row, moving from left to right. For example, if the classroom is structured with shapes and colors representing areas or activities, the pockets will hold corresponding shapes and colors. Lilly, who has already learned to go to the one-to-one teaching area when she is handed the red circle, will now be taught to look at her row on the pocket chart, take the red circle out of the first pocket, and move to the red-circle area of the classroom.

One benefit of using the pocket chart to organize children's schedules is its flexibility. Children's schedules can be changed quickly by removing a colored shape, icon, or photo and replacing it with another. In addition, the schedule makes it easier to teach children step by step. They learn to do one activity on the schedule, then two, then three or more. As they become more independent, children with autism/PDD will not have to be verbally directed, cued, or physically guided as often. There should be fewer instances of resistance as children learn to follow directions that are part of a daily routine.

Children who do not need to use colors or symbols can use a pocket-chart schedule with photographs of activities, specific toys or learning tools, and locations in the classroom or school. If children respond to icons better than photos, then icons can be used. Regardless of what specific symbols are used to establish the pocket-chart schedules, it is important that the teacher show the child

the card, clearly say and repeat the name of the activity, guide the child to take the card out of the pocket, and then take the child to the activity. This sequence should be repeated until the child can follow his or her schedule independently. Start with just the photograph of the child and one activity, and then add other activities one at a time. For example, Rusty can find his photograph on the pocket chart, take out the photo of the gross-motor, large-toy area, and go to that section of the classroom on his own.

Use a strip schedule.

Sometimes children have motor problems that prevent them from removing a card from the pocket chart or they might not begin the process willingly. To avoid a prolonged struggle, back up and use a simple strip of sturdy poster board or cardboard with two Velcro squares. A small strip schedule is often a first step to independence, and more advanced systems can be introduced later.

Constructing a strip schedule is easy. Cut a piece of cardboard or sturdy poster board into a convenient size and shape. (A rectangle of about 4″ × 8″ is usually a good size for a very young child.) Draw a line in the middle of the rectangle from top to bottom, so that you have two 4″ × 4″ squares. Laminate the rectangle and place two Velcro squares in the middle of each half of the strip. Next, place the child's photograph on the first square, so that he  knows it is his schedule. Then next to the photo, place a picture of the activity, location, or person on his schedule. For example, Caleb's schedule has his picture and a picture of the playground on it. His first assigned activity is an imitation lesson that will take place outside on the playground with his teacher. When Caleb has learned to use his schedule strip for one activity, his teacher will add more sections and items to his schedule.

Teach children how to use visual schedules.

When you are teaching a young child with autism/PDD to use simple schedules with line drawings, photographs, icons, or objects, it is helpful to start the process with an activity the child enjoys. Establishing the connection between the visual cue and the activity may take many repetitions, but the process is likely to go more quickly if the activity presented is one that the child prefers. If we know that Rusty loves eating ice cream, we will show him a photograph of a bowl of ice cream, then immediately walk him to the table, help him sit down, and present him with a small dish of ice cream. To reinforce verbal language, we would also cue him with the words, "ice cream." Rusty should quickly learn that the picture of ice cream represents the activity of eating ice cream.

While this sequence is simple and seems obvious, it is important that it be repeated often for the young child with autism/PDD to understand the meaning

of the picture (e.g., a photo of ice cream represents the ice cream, a small bowl and spoon represents the ice cream, or a drawing of a bowl of ice cream represents the ice cream). The adults in this situation must keep in mind that in addition to teaching the connection between the abstract representation and the actual object, they are also teaching the child to do whatever activity is presented to him visually (i.e., to follow his or her schedule).

This type of simple schedule can also be used at home. When teaching children new skills that they may resist at first, start with a nonpreferred (work) activity, then follow it with a preferred (play) activity. This type of alternating schedule also may be called a 1/2, First/Then, or Now/Next system (a blank form is provided in Appendix 4, p. 67). When young children begin to understand that they will get to do what they want only if they do what you want first, they often become more cooperative very quickly. However, as with any system, even this simple approach should be used as consistently as possible and taught to the child throughout the day. Visuals, objects, photographs, or icons that represent all of the activities, people, places, and things in the child's schedule should be readily available.

Remember that when a young child who has autism/PDD learns to follow a schedule, he or she is also learning independence, following directions, matching, and understanding the connection between symbols and their meanings, skills that are essential for language development.

Calendars

You will see examples of some basic calendars in this section. Blank versions of these are provided in Appendix 4 at the end of the chapter. These simple calendars are designed to address a specific need or to communicate specific information. While they are very basic, calendars like these are helpful with very young children who become agitated when things change, who do not transition smoothly from one person or situation to the next, or who have problems understanding the sequence of their activities. Teaching a young child to understand a calendar requires teaching the meaning of events and then establishing the association between the real events and their representations. Because young children have a limited understanding of time, we suggest using two basic calendars to begin teaching them how calendars work—a home/school calendar and a people calendar.

Create home/school calendars.

Young children with autism/PDD may need help learning the association between events and their visual representations, so start your calendar with a limited number of events that are clearly differentiated from each other. One simple way to start the process is to teach the child about his or her daily events. A first step is to teach the difference between the child's two primary environments, home and school.

Start with a simple calendar that includes two photographs, drawings, or icons—one that represents home and one that represents school. Present them in alternating order before going to either place. For example, each night, before going to bed, Lilly's parents show her either the icon representing school or the icon representing home. They tell her, "Tomorrow is school," or "Tomorrow is home." Then they place the icon at eye level by her door, so she sees it first thing the next morning. When Lilly gets up in the morning, her parents show her one of the two icons and tell her, "Today is school," or "Today is home." Likewise, before she leaves school to go home, her teacher shows her the icon for the

next day. So, if it's Friday, she tells Lilly, "Tomorrow is home," and shows her the home icon. This simple system, used consistently both at home and at school, is an essential first step for Lilly in learning to understand a calendar. After several months, the teacher may introduce a weekly calendar, with seven icons, beginning with the "school" icon on Monday and showing five "schools" and two "homes."

Remember that weeks and months probably seem like endless periods of time for young children, especially those with autism/PDD. While some calendars can be used for instruction on a daily basis, expecting a very young child with autism to track an entire week or month is probably unrealistic unless you start with the basic calendars described above.

Use people calendars.

Visual calendars can also be used to communicate to very young children about which people they will see throughout the day. There are often many people coming and going in the lives of young children with autism/PDD and some are more likely to meet resistance or cause anxiety than others. People calendars, whether on a pocket chart or a strip schedule, can minimize the child's uncertainty and prevent transition difficulties. People calendars can include one person at a time (i.e., the next person the child will see) or show everyone he or she will see that day.

For example, on Monday, Lilly is going to see her bus driver, Ms. Jones, first. Next, she will see her preschool teacher, Ms. Franklin, who usually greets her as she gets off the bus. The next adult Lilly will see is Mr. Cantu, one of the teaching assistants in the preschool class. Lilly will also see the other students in her class.

Her calendar shows these four photos. Lilly's parents and her teacher will teach Lilly her schedule, review it several times during the day, and ensure that she knows everyone whom she will see. We have provided several simple forms in Appendix 4 that can easily be used for people calendars.

As you may already understand from reading Chapters 2 through 4, every component of the educational program for young children with autism is important. Each component is also essential in providing the framework for the next step. After creating and using a visual framework for communication, structuring the environment, and developing schedules, you can turn your attention to establishing routines and teaching skills. Children will learn routines and skills more quickly if the other components of the program are already in place and used consistently.

Supporting References and Resources

Bryan, L. C., & Gast, D. L. (2000). Teaching on-task and on-schedule behaviors to high-functioning children with autism via picture activity schedules. *Journal of Autism and Developmental Disorders, 30*(6), 553–567.

Carothers, D. E., & Taylor, R. L. (2004). How teachers and parents can work together to teach daily living skills to children with autism. *Focus on Autism & Other Developmental Disabilities, 19*(2), 102–104.

Crum, C. F. (2004). Using a cognitive-behavioral modification strategy to increase on-task behavior of a student with a behavior disorder. *Intervention in School and Clinic, 39*(5), 305–309.

Dalrymple, N. J. (1995). Environmental supports to develop flexibility and independence. In K. Quill (Ed.), *Teaching children with autism* (pp. 243–264). New York: Delmar.

De Hass-Warner, S. (1992). The utility of self-monitoring for preschool on-task behavior. *Topics in Early Childhood Special Education, 12*(4), 478–495.

Earles, T. L., Carlson, J. K., & Bock, S. J. (1998). Instructional strategies to facilitate successful learning outcomes for students with autism. In R. L. Simpson & B. S. Myles (Eds.), *Educating children and youth with autism: Strategies for effective practice* (pp. 55–111). Austin, TX: PRO-ED.

Hardin, L. R., & Howard, V. F. (1993). Using self-recording of on-task behavior by a preschool child with disabilities. *Perceptual & Motor Skills, 77*(3), 786.

Koegel, L. K., Stiebel, D., & Koegel, R. L. (1987). The influence of child-preferred activities on autistic children's social behavior. *Journal of Applied Behavior Analysis, 20*(3), 243–252.

McDuff, G. S., Krantz, P. J., & McClannahan, L. E. (1993). Teaching children with autism to use photographic activity schedules: Maintenance and generalization of complex response chains. *Journal of Applied Behavior Analysis, 26,* 89–97.

CHAPTER 4 APPENDIX

Reproducible Forms

Morning Lesson Plans

Teacher's Name _____   Date _____

	Monday	Tuesday	Wednesday	Thursday	Friday
8:00					
8:30					
9:00					
9:30					
10:00					
10:30					
11:00					
11:30					

Afternoon Lesson Plans

Teacher's Name _____   Date _____

	Monday	Tuesday	Wednesday	Thursday	Friday
12:00					
12:30					
1:00					
1:30					
2:00					
2:30					
3:00					
3:30					

Schedule

Student's Name _____   Date _____

1 _____

2 _____

3 _____

4 _____

5 _____

6 _____

7 _____

8 _____

Our Morning Schedule

Time	Related Services	Teacher _____	Aide/Para. _____
7:45			
8:00			
8:15			
8:30			
8:45			
9:00			
9:15			
9:30			
9:45			
10:00			
10:15			
10:30			
10:45			
11:00			
11:15			
11:30			
11:45			

Our Afternoon Schedule

Time	Related Services	Teacher _____	Aide/Para. _____
12:00			
12:15			
12:30			
12:45			
1:00			
1:15			
1:30			
1:45			
2:00			
2:15			
2:30			
2:45			
3:00			
3:15			
3:30			
3:45			
4:00			

Schedule

Time	Teacher _____	Paraprofessional _____	Paraprofessional _____

Daily Schedule

Time	Group 1	Group 2	Group 3

Home

School

Weekly Calendar

Monday	Tuesday	Wednesday	Thursday	Friday	Saturday	Sunday
School	School	School	School	School	Home	Home

Daily Schedule

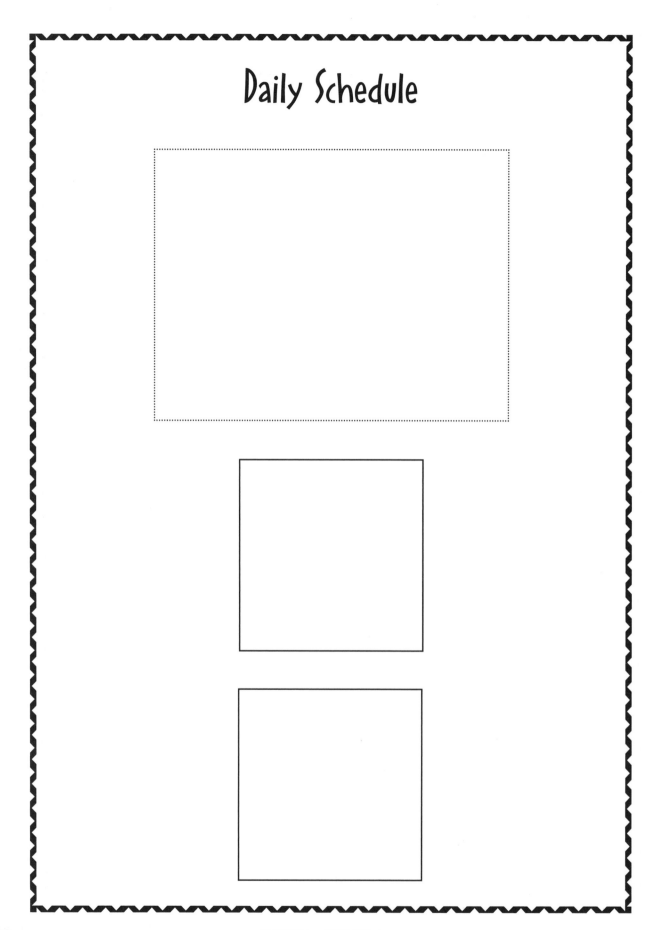

Daily Schedule

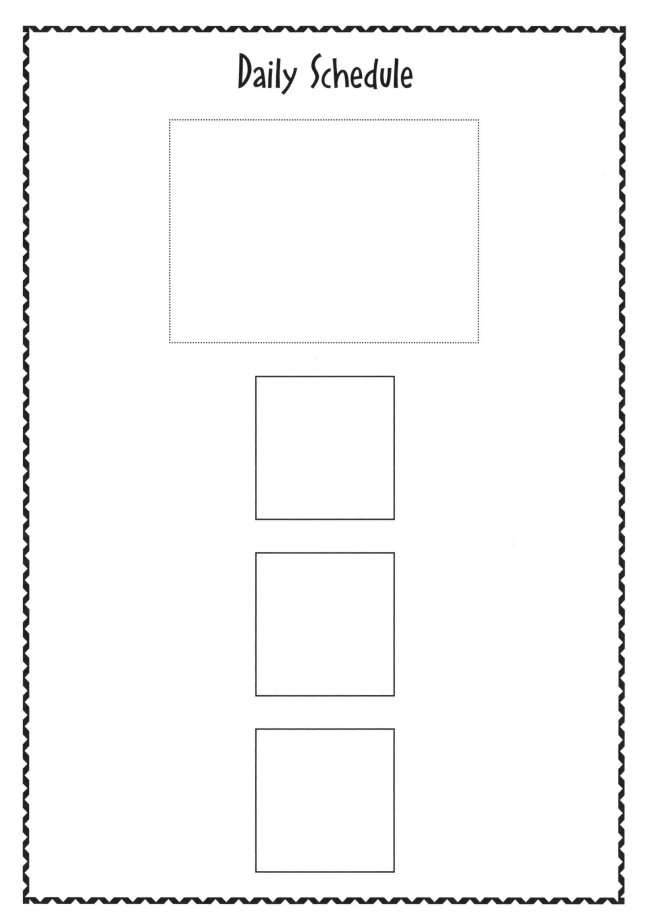

Daily Schedule

5 Establish and Teach Routines

Many types of instruction can be effective when teaching young children with autism/PDD, including the direct teaching of specific skills and incidental teaching that occurs all day long when opportunities arise. One strategy for teaching young children involves establishing and teaching routines and then using those routines to teach additional skills. This chapter provides the following information:

- Using guidelines to establish and teach routines

- Establishing and teaching typical daily routines at home and school

- Using a planning process and form to help structure instruction

- Identifying additional skills that can be targeted

Guidelines

For young children, instruction involving routines is an age-appropriate technique that can be used in all environments. Whether a young child is in day care, at home, in a preschool classroom, participating in a play group, or working with a therapist, predictable activities should be in place. Routines help young children learn and develop independence. Use the following guidelines to establish and teach routines.

Use repetition to help children learn.

One way that we master information is to repeat it—say it often, do it often, and practice until we have memorized it and "know it by heart." Teaching routines to children while they are young can help them establish a pattern of behavior and learn the connections among all components of the routines, including the time of day, location, purpose, actions, cues, and language involved. With careful attention to the level of prompting and cueing, as well as the communication involved, young children should learn to anticipate what they need to do and do it more easily. For example, Rusty's teacher uses the same routine at snack time every day:

① Put away materials

② Wash hands

③ Sit at table

④ Wait for snack

When repeated each day, this routine, over time, will help Rusty learn to get ready for snack time independently.

Teach routines to develop independence.

Routines allow young children to initiate actions, rather than always being directed, told, or guided to do something. Initiating behaviors is both a difficult and important skill for young children with autism/PDD. It is difficult because so many children with autism are passive or dependent on others for direction. As long as this is the case, they are unlikely to interact independently and effectively with people or objects in their environment. Initiating an activity is so important because it facilitates additional learning. When children consistently sit back and wait for someone to tell them what to do and when they fail to demonstrate curiosity, their rate of learning is likely to be slow. Children who learn only during direct instruction miss out on all the learning that takes place in the ordinary exchanges between people during daily living.

The last example described Rusty's snack routine at school. At home, Rusty's mother is anxious for Rusty to generalize his learned routine to home. If he walks to the kitchen sink and washes his hands before a snack without being told, it will be clear that he has not just learned a skill but can initiate the behavior independently in another setting. This generalization and subsequent independence are critical for Rusty's success in life.

Establish predictable routines.

Predictable routines provide young children with autism/PDD consistency and safety. Most of us crave a measure of stability and familiarity in our lives. If we had to deal with unfamiliar and potentially frightening situations constantly, we would no doubt experience stress and anxiety. However, most of us can tolerate some change, some unfamiliar situations, and some unexpected events. For the young child with autism/PDD, the ability to tolerate change and deal with the unexpected is often limited. Transitions, novel people or circumstances, and unexpected changes are a challenge. Routines have the potential to make life go more smoothly not just for children but for their parents and teachers as well. Although change is difficult for Lilly, her teacher and parents have found that if they use predictable routines, including consistent visual and verbal cues, she is better able to tolerate change when it happens. Lilly's parents always stick to a predictable pattern when they get ready to get in the car:

① Put on shoes

② Get "To Do" bag

③ Hold Mom's or Dad's hand when walking to the car

Use routines to teach desired behaviors.

Routines help prevent behavior problems. When young children are presented with an activity designed to be completed independently, they often need guidance or direction to complete it. Young children with autism/PDD may have trouble with independent tasks

because they often do not attend to directions and do not understand what is required of them. For these reasons, teaching routines, repeating verbal and activity sequences, and building predictable patterns of behavior are important and useful to the young child with autism. The teaching can employ several methods, including the steps explained in this chapter. Instructing a child in expected behaviors shows that these skills can and should be taught, rather than just expected.

Consistent instruction designed to teach desired behaviors should focus on socially appropriate behaviors that will be expected as children get older. For example, Caleb sometimes resists when he is asked to get out of his parent's car when he arrives at school. His refusals are both passive (he just sits and will refuse to get up) and active (he hits and kicks at his parents if they try to remove him from his car seat). However, teaching him the routine of following his parents' directions to leave the car when it arrives at the curb at school may prevent later refusals. Caleb's teacher and his parents have worked together to create a four-step "leave the car" routine:

① Get unbuckled

② Climb out of the car

③ Wave good-bye

④ Take the teacher's hand

Caleb's signal to start the sequence of getting out of the car is a "Follow Mom and Dad's Directions" card. His parents show him this card first, and then present him with the picture cues for the four steps in the sequence. After he has taken his teacher's hand, she praises him and gives him a token for following directions. Teaching Caleb the signal to get ready to

follow directions sets the stage for him to follow many other directions throughout his life. Parents and teachers can use this cue whenever they teach any new skill. It is critical for Caleb's teacher to praise him and use positive reinforcement when he follows directions, regardless of what the direction is. This is how he will learn that following directions is important and valued by the adults in his environment.

Use routines to encourage joint attention and imitation.

The term "joint attention" describes a situation in which two or more participants are looking at the same thing at the same time. Two people who are jointly attending, whether looking at the pages of a book, watching a TV show, or playing a game, also tend to "check" with each other. This may involve occasionally looking at each other to gauge reaction, evaluate responses, or imitate expressions and language. Because of this tendency to check with each other and sometimes mimic the other person's responses, joint attending often becomes the basis of imitation, one of the most basic and most efficient ways to learn new information.

Joint attending and imitation are considered critical to communication and are often referred to as core skills (i.e., skills that are essential for the development of other communication and behavioral competencies). There is a comprehensive body of research that not only validates the importance of these two core skills for communication development in young children, but also shows that these two skills are frequently a problem for children with autism/PDD. The interrelationship between joint attention and imitation makes it even more important for adults who work with young children who have autism/PDD to address these two core skills. Mastery of one (joint attention) may maximize mastery of the other (imitation).

Although both joint attention and imitation are often difficult for children with autism/PDD, the good news is that both skills can improve, especially when they are systematically taught and reinforced. During the process of establishing and teaching with routines, adults and children should focus simultaneously on the visuals used to explain the steps of the routine, the objects used in the routine, and the language used to "talk the child through" his or her actions. Lilly is learning a new skill through joint attention and imitation. Although Lilly has some very strong skills, she is still having difficulty learning language. Her teacher has been teaching Lilly a routine for requesting her lunch in the cafeteria. She has learned to point to the items she wants and repeat a sequence that begins with the commonly used sentence starter, "I want . . . ." Lilly has repeated the routine so many times that without any prompting or visual cues, she now says, "I want juice" and "I want milk" independently. In addition, she will request several other items when prompted (apple, burger, cookie).

The routine has taught Lilly to use a consistent pattern of communication to get what she wants. Teaching the routine involved modeling each step, giving visual and verbal cues, and having Lilly imitate, all of which were taught systematically and repeated numerous times. Because her teacher has clearly defined Lilly's goals and is consistent in her teaching methods, Lilly learns more quickly than she would through just prompting or cueing alone.

Steps

Teaching routines can be successful for many children with autism/PDD when a few specific steps are followed.

Identify daily routines and assess performance level.

The first step in teaching is to determine your objective, or what it is you want to teach. Begin by identifying the child's typical daily routines and how much support is needed for him or her to complete them. When selecting routines to use as part of your instructional program, consider everything that happens during the child's day, especially activities that are important to adults. Remember that even the simplest tasks can be used as teaching opportunities and that those repeated most often have great potential. The lists that follow provide examples of many typical home and school routines; however, almost anything a young child does on a daily basis can be taught using a sequence that is repeated.

Typical Home Routines for Young Children

- Waking up and getting out of bed
- Getting dressed
- Eating breakfast
- Grooming (brushing teeth/combing hair)
- Leaving the house
- Getting into the car or bus
- Putting on the seatbelt and riding in the car
- Getting out of the car
- Saying good-bye and leaving

- Getting off the bus or out of car after returning home
- Taking off coat and hanging it up
- Putting school materials away
- Having a snack or drink
- Choosing toys
- Playing/Stopping play
- Watching TV/Stopping TV
- Getting undressed/Dressing in pajamas
- Brushing teeth
- Taking a bath
- Listening to a story
- Getting in bed
- Saying goodnight

Typical School Routines for Young Children

- Getting off the bus or out of the car
- Greeting adults
- Entering school
- Entering the classroom
- Hanging up coat and backpack
- Greeting classmates and adults
- Sitting down
- Checking calendar or schedule
- Getting ready to work in small group
- Getting ready to work alone
- Waiting
- Asking for help
- Starting a new activity
- Stopping an activity
- Moving from one place to another in school
- Getting ready for a snack
- Having lunch

- Finishing an activity
- Picking up toys and materials
- Getting ready to go home
- Walking to the bus or car
- Saying good-bye
- Getting on bus or in car

These routines are presented again at the end of the chapter in Appendix 5 as two checklists. Next to each routine are four columns, indicating whether the child cannot perform the routine at all, needs much help to do it, needs a little help to do it, or can complete the routine without help. Completing these forms will help school personnel know what the child can do at home and family members know what routines are expected at school. Once the information on the forms has been reviewed, goals and objectives can easily be identified.

Decide which routines to teach.

After the child's current performance level on specific routines has been assessed, the educational team can then decide which ones should be established or taught first. The decision about which routines to focus on will depend on several factors, including the answers to the following questions:

- Which routines are most critical for the child's independence?
  (For example, Lilly getting her food in the cafeteria.)

- Which routines are most important to communicate needs?
  (For example, Rusty asking for his snack at school.)

- Which routines are necessary to prevent disruptive or dangerous behaviors?
  (For example, Caleb getting out of the car without a tantrum.)

- Which routines are prerequisites to learning other skills?
  (For example, Rusty's getting a snack at school, which leads to his getting his own snack at home.)

Following are some key points to remember when selecting routines to teach.

Simplicity

A young child with autism/PDD is likely to be overwhelmed or confused if he or she is subjected to instruction on a wide variety of skills that have different expectations throughout the day. Choose one to three routines at first. If three is too many, cut back to just one or two. Once the target routines have been selected, systematic instruction to teach the routines at school and home can begin.

Consistency

Learning occurs more quickly when skills are taught consistently and reinforced each time they are demonstrated. When routines are taught in a preschool class, it is essential that the teacher and any instructional assistants or paraprofessionals all teach the same skill the same way. To maintain consistency, weekly staffings or short daily meetings should be held so that all personel understand the steps of each routine, how they will be taught, and what reinforcer will follow. Begin with routines that occur often, so that they can be taught and practiced many times throughout the day.

Create a simple plan.

In teaching routines, instructional planning is essential but plans must be kept simple if teachers, support personnel, parents, and others are to understand and follow the plan. The following key guidelines should help team members teach routines to young children. These guidelines are also presented on the Routine Planning Form at the end of this chapter. Because teaching young children requires a high level of active involvement from adults, the planning form has been kept simple, and the steps in the teaching plan are very straightforward.

Words and Visuals

Use both words and a visual representation. This information can be written in the *What* section of the Routine Planning Form. Refer back to the previous lists (Typical Home Routines for Young Children and Typical School Routines for Young Children), then review the criteria mentioned above. Start with routines that are essential for independence, important for communication, necessary to prevent behavior problems, and are prerequisites for other skills. In some cases, beginning to establish even very simple routines will be a challenge.

When beginning to teach a routine to a young child, include only two or three steps. For example, an instructional routine for Caleb is called Get Ready To Work. If we use our Routine Planning Form, the visual representation of Get Ready To Work for Caleb will be placed in the top box on the right side of the form and the words in the blank in the left column.

Steps

Again, simple is better. Remember that success is the goal. It is much better to begin teaching only one or two simple skills first. Once those skills are mastered and the child has been successful demonstrating them, set a goal that either adds a new skill to an established routine or begins to teach a new routine. Because Caleb's rate of learning is slow, we would like to teach him three steps to help him *get ready to work*. The steps we originally proposed are:

① Sit

② Listen

③ Do

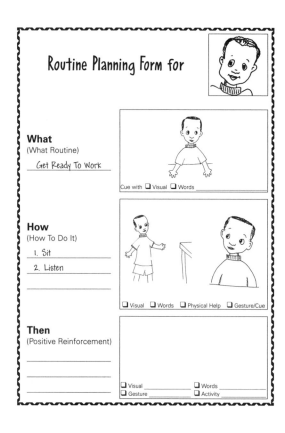

Routine Planning Form for

What
(What Routine)
Get Ready To Work

Cue with ❑ Visual ❑ Words _____

How
(How To Do It)
_____
_____
_____

❑ Visual ❑ Words ❑ Physical Help ❑ Gesture/Cue

Then
(Positive Reinforcement)
_____
_____
_____

❑ Visual _____ ❑ Words
❑ Gesture _____ ❑ Activity

Routine Planning Form for

What
(What Routine)
Get Ready To Work

Cue with ❑ Visual ❑ Words _____

How
(How To Do It)
1. Sit
2. Listen
_____

❑ Visual ❑ Words ❑ Physical Help ❑ Gesture/Cue

Then
(Positive Reinforcement)
_____
_____
_____

❑ Visual _____ ❑ Words
❑ Gesture _____ ❑ Activity

After discussion during a staffing, however, the team may decide that Caleb is not ready for the *Do* step because he has not mastered basic attending skills. In that case, we will simplify the routine to a two-step process emphasizing just the attending skills:

① Sit

② Listen

Once Caleb can sit and listen, we will add Step 3, *Do.*

To complete the Routine Planning Form, the team should again choose visuals to represent the routine, this time identifying the specific steps (Sit, Listen). This planning step is important because everyone on the team, including parents, should be teaching Caleb the Get Ready To Work routine, and if Caleb doesn't know what steps are expected of him when given that direction, he will be confused and slow to master it.

Prompting

There are several terms used to describe prompting and definitions of the terms vary. Whether you use the term *prompting, cueing, guidance, assistance,* or something else, the team must decide how much prompting everyone will use when teaching the steps of the routine. Teaching a brand-new skill to a young child will usually require a lot of direct prompting. Once the skill is learned, maintenance should require less obvious prompting. Always use caution if physically prompting a young child. Children are small and weak compared to adults and are often powerless to protect themselves. We urge adults to use little or no physical prompting and then only when it strictly conforms to legal and ethical guidelines. In addition to physical risks, the child may also become dependent on the physical prompt, which will completely undermine the process of teaching him or her to complete a routine independently.

Caleb's team decided that they would use three levels of prompting simultaneously when first teaching him the routine Get Ready To Work: words, visual cues,

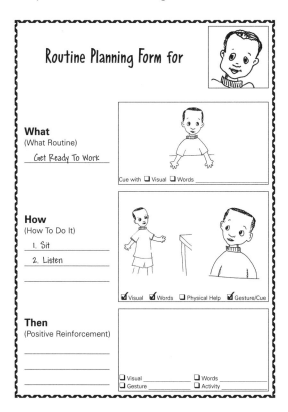

and a gesture. For the first step, *Sit*, they will show Caleb the visual for sit, say "Sit", and point to the chair. For *Listen*, they will show the visual for listen, say "Listen," and point to their ears with their thumb and open hand (similar to the American Sign Language sign for listen). When filling in the Routine Planning Form, the team will check the boxes in the How section that indicate words, visual, and gesture/cue.

Later, the team should be able reduce the level of prompting, either by omitting the gesture, the visual, or both, and just saying, "Sit."

Teaching Sequence

The second page of the Routine Planning Form should help you decide on the teaching sequence. This page presents the basic steps for teaching a young child with autism/PDD: cueing to gain the child's attention, looking to ensure joint attention, modeling the individual steps of the routine, waiting so that the child has ample opportunity to demonstrate the step in the routine, watching to make sure the child does what he or she is supposed to do, and providing positive reinforcement. As you design the teaching sequence, keep the following key principles in mind. Each of these should be a team effort.

Cue. Decide on the cue that will be used to let the child know the routine is about to begin. As we have suggested before, it is best to keep things simple. For example, to tell Caleb that we want him to Get Ready To Work, we will simply show him the visual cue and say, "Caleb, get ready to work." Even though this is simple, we want to make sure that everyone on the team understands what to do and say, so we will write this information in the first box on page 1 of the Routine Planning Form and in Item 1 on the second page of the form.

Record. Plan to record how well the child does when learning a new routine. The frequency of recording will depend on several factors, including the difficulty of the routine, the number of repetitions that the team thinks are necessary, and the phase of instruction (i.e., teaching a brand-new skill or maintaining an already learned skill). Strategies for collecting and recording data are explained in Chapter 7.

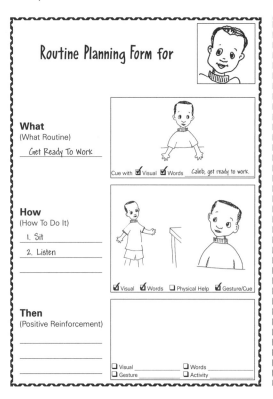

Reinforce. Reinforce the child after he or she demonstrates the steps of the routine. Because many of the routines of young children are repeated often throughout the day and do not take much time, physical gestures and words are usually the most effective means of positive reinforcement. It takes very little time to praise a child and give a thumbs-up sign. When words and gestures are used consistently and with enthusiasm, they are effective at increasing the occurrence of specific behaviors. Young children with autism/PDD may not always reciprocate when presented with verbal and social reinforcement like praise, smiles, and signals, but evidence shows that this type of positive reinforcement works.

In our example, the team has decided to use all four of the types of reinforcement listed on the form when Caleb demonstrates the steps in his Get Ready To Work routine. The teacher and the teaching assistants are going to smile (a physical gesture), say, "Great sitting" or "Great listening" (words), show him the picture of playdough (visual), and then let him play with playdough (activity), his favorite material for play time. They will do these almost simultaneously, so that Caleb connects what he has just done with their actions. In this example, using an activity as reinforcement should be effective, because the work Caleb is getting ready for in his Get Ready To Work routine will be something he enjoys and wants to do anyway. The team can now complete the remaining sections of the Routine Planning Form, the box on the bottom of page 1 and Item 6 on page 2.

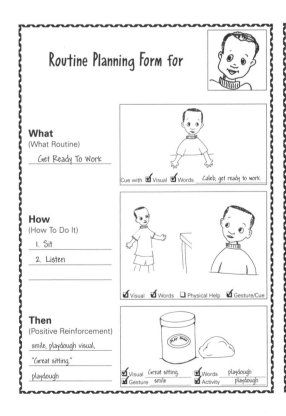

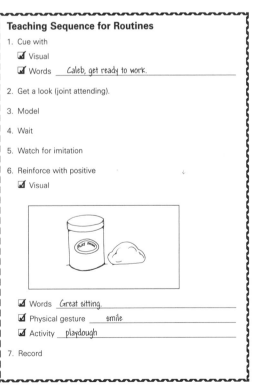

Consistent Pattern

Earlier, we discussed the importance of consistency when teaching young children. It will help the adults on the team as well as the young child with autism/PDD if routines are established and taught in all environments, at many different times throughout the day by a variety of individuals. The child will learn more rapidly and generalize the skills more easily. Team planning can ensure that all individuals who work with the child use the same teaching sequence and record the child's progress. As one routine is mastered, another should be taught that builds on the existing routine or teaches a brand-new skill.

Independence

At the beginning of the chapter, we discussed the reasons for teaching routines to young children with autism/PDD. Among the most important goals for this type of instruction are increased independence and mastery of new skills. To ensure that these two goals are met, it is necessary to reduce the level of adult participation in the routine. This can be done several ways.

Reduce Cueing. To reduce the amount of cueing before the routine, adults will need to practice some creative waiting. Instead of actively directing the child when it's the normal time to complete a routine, just wait. Let the child take the

initiative and begin the first steps of the routine on his or her own. If the child tries to get adult attention, ask what he or she wants, pretend you don't understand, or look puzzled. Give the child a chance to function independently. If Caleb will get ready to work with only a verbal direction and doesn't require a visual cue anymore, we will happily eliminate the use of the visual cue. Then, when Caleb has begun to sit when it's time to work, we will stop using the visual and verbal directions.

Reduce Assistance. Reduce the level of assistance provided during the routine by using less prompting, fewer visual cues, more subtle gestures, or fewer words. Unless adults make a systematic effort to reduce their control of routine situations, many young children with autism/PDD are unlikely to complete tasks on their own. In our efforts to support and assist children, we sometimes promote their helplessness. Any reduction in assistance should be planned by the team and implemented systematically. Information regarding the impact of

reduced prompting should be recorded and reviewed regularly. Once Caleb's team has decided that he doesn't need us to gesture to his ears when we say, "Listen," then his teacher no longer uses that physical signal with him. He is alert and ready to listen when the teacher says, "Listen" and shows him his visual cue. Later, Caleb should be ready to listen after just a verbal direction.

Reduce Reinforcement. Reduce the frequency or quality of the positive reinforcement provided. Changes to positive reinforcement often occur naturally. When children first master skills, we are excited and call attention to every instance of their success. As they continue to demonstrate established behaviors, we become accustomed to them and provide less enthusiastic or less frequent reinforcement. For young children who have autism/PDD, however, positive reinforcement is one of our most important tools for teaching new skills. Any changes in reinforcement should be part of a comprehensive review of the child's program.

Examples of changes to positive reinforcement include: using reinforcement later in the routine, after additional steps are completed; using reinforcement at the end of the routine instead of during the routine; reinforcing each step only if it is done completely independently; and using fewer activities as reinforcers and more social praise, because praise and compliments are more typically available and natural in everyday life. In Caleb's case, his teacher wants him to do both steps of the Get Ready To Work routine in rapid succession (i.e., sit and listen without pausing). Once she thinks Caleb can succeed under these conditions, she may postpone the playdough activity until he completes both steps independently.

Regardless of the strategies used to promote greater independence in routine daily activities, it is critical that decision-making include all team members. Strategies should be communicated clearly and practiced to ensure consistency. We teach routines so that children can eventually complete those routines on their own, thereby achieving another step toward independence.

Additional Skills

Teachers who use the Routine Planning Form to teach routines to young children with autism/PDD identify specific steps in the routine as part of the planning process. In addition, teachers may also wish to target other skills and address those during instruction. We have provided a form called Target Skills for a Specific Routine that can be used to help professionals and parents plan. After teaching a specific routine, additional skills can be emphasized during the routine. These skills are then taught, not in isolation, but as part of an already established pattern. The key is that everyone on the team is aware of what skills to emphasize and reinforce.

For example, when we taught Caleb to Get Ready To Work, we decided to teach two behaviors in that routine: Sit and Listen. However, Caleb's speech–language therapist, Ms. Thomas, has also identified several communication goals for Caleb. One of those goals is making eye contact. Ms. Thomas noted that Step 2 in the Get Ready To Work teaching sequence (Get a Look) is similar to her speech–language goal of eye contact. She asked everyone on Caleb's team to make sure that when they teach his Get Ready To Work routine, they emphasize the Get a Look step. Ms. Thomas has shown each team member some ways to prompt eye contact (e.g., holding an object by her eye, getting close to Caleb and looking directly at his eyes). Ms. Thomas also explained the importance of eye contact to Caleb's parents and suggested they emphasize eye contact from him at home before they give him a direction. Eye contact from your child is always desirable, and it is a good indicator that he or she is listening and ready to comply.

An infinite number of skills can be targeted when teaching routines. But again, we suggest that teams working with children who have autism/PDD focus their attention on a small number of skills at one time. On the form we have provided, teams can identify three additional goals in each of the areas in the *Diagnostic and Statistical Manual of Mental Disorders, Fourth Edition–Text Revision (DSM–IV–TR)* definition of autism: social interaction, communication, and behavior: repetitive/stereotyped patterns.

To select skills that can be integrated into and taught during instruction in routines, we suggest using the Evaluation Form from an earlier publication by the same authors: *Practical Ideas That Really Work for Students with Autism Spectrum Disorders*. While not all of the items on this evaluation form will apply to young children, the form does list specific skills that are directly linked to the criteria for autism found in

Target Skills for a Specific Routine

Name of Student _____ *Caleb* _____

Routine ___ *Get Ready To Work* _____

Required Target Skills ___ *sit, listen* _____

Additional Target Skills That Can Be Taught in This Routine

Social Interaction Skills ___ *Sit facing another person* ___

_____

_____

Communication Skills ___ *Make eye contact* ___

_____

_____

Behavior Skills
(Repetitive/Stereotyped)
Follow the directions ___

Keep hands quiet ___

_____

DSM–IV–TR. A section of the Communication items on that form are shown on the following page. There are many other skills checklists that can be used when targeting specific skills for instruction, and additional information is provided in the next chapter on direct instruction. By using a thorough planning and instructional model, preschoolers with autism/PDD can master key skills faster, learning how to learn as they do so. Not only will Caleb get ready for work when asked, hopefully he will enjoy his work activities and respond quickly and positively to the next routine he is taught.

BEHAVIOR	RATING			
	Not at all	*Somewhat*	*Very much*	*Exactly*
Communication				
Expressive Language				
1 Does not speak spontaneously to others.	0	1	2	3
2 Does not use gestures or signs to communicate with others.	0	1	2	3
3 Does not let others know through words or gestures his or her needs or desires.	0	1	2	3
Conversation (Only rate if student has spoken language.)				
1 Does not initiate conversations with others.	0	1	2	3
2 Fails to use greetings (e.g., hello) or courteous phrases (e.g., please, thank you).	0	1	2	3
3 Does not ask others' questions.	0	1	2	3
Stereotyped Language (Only rate if student has spoken language.)				
1 Echolalic (i.e., repeats what he or she hears, rather than responding appropriately).	0	1	2	3
2 Perseverates (i.e., repeats the same phrase over and over).	0	1	2	3
3 Recites common phrases heard on television or radio.	0	1	2	3

Note. From *Practical Ideas That Really Work for Students with Autism Spectrum Disorders*, by K. McConnell and G. Ryser, 2000, Austin, TX: PRO-ED, Inc. Copyright 2000 by PRO-ED, Inc. Reprinted with permission.

Supporting References and Resources

American Psychiatric Association. (2000). *Diagnostic and statistical manual of mental disorders* (4th ed., Text Rev.). Washington, DC: Author.

Christodulu, K. V., & Durand, V. M. (2004). Reducing bedtime disturbance and night waking using positive bedtime routines and sleep restriction. *Focus on Autism and Other Developmental Disabilities, 19*(3), 130–139.

Dawson, G., Toth, K., Abott, R., Osterling, J., Munson, J., Estes, A., & et al. (2004). Early social attention impairments in autism: Social orienting, joint attention and attention to distress. *Developmental Psychology, 40*(2), 271–283.

Fisher, W., Piazza, C. C., Bowman, L. G., Hagopian, L. P., Owens, J. C., & Slevin, I. (1992). A comparison of two approaches for identifying reinforcers for persons with severe and profound disabilities. *Journal of Applied Behavior Analysis, 25,* 491–498.

Ingersoll, B., Schreibman, L., & Tran, Q. (2003). Effect of sensory feedback on immediate object imitation in children with autism. *Journal of Autism & Developmental Disorders, 33*(6), 673–683.

Jones, E. A., & Carr, E. G. (2004). Joint attention in children with autism: Theory and intervention. *Focus on Autism and Other Developmental Disabilities, 19*(1), 13–26.

McConnell, K., & Ryser, G. (2000). Practical ideas that really work for students with autism spectrum disorders. Austin, TX: PRO-ED.

Soorya, L. V., Arnstein, L. M., Gillis, J., & Romanczyk, R. G. (2003). An overview of imitation skills in autism: Implications for practice. *The Behavior Analyst Today, 4*(2), 114–123.

Woods, J., & Goldstein, H. (2003). When the toddler takes over: Changing challenging routines into conduits for communication. *Focus on Autism and Other Developmental Disabilities, 18*(3), 176–181.

CHAPTER 5 APPENDIX

Reproducible Forms

Typical Home Routines

	Cannot Do It	Needs Much Help	Needs Little Help	Can Do It
• Waking up and getting out of bed				
• Getting dressed				
• Eating breakfast				
• Grooming (brushing teeth/combing hair)				
• Leaving the house				
• Getting into the car or bus				
• Putting on the seatbelt and riding in the car				
• Getting out of the car				
• Saying good-bye and leaving				
• Getting off the bus or out of car after returning home				
• Taking off coat and hanging it up				
• Putting school materials away				
• Having a snack or drink				
• Choosing toys				
• Playing/Stopping play				
• Watching TV/Stopping TV				
• Getting undressed/Dressing in pajamas				
• Brushing teeth				
• Taking a bath				
• Listening to a story				
• Getting in to bed				
• Saying goodnight				

Typical School Routines

	Cannot Do It	Needs Much Help	Needs Little Help	Can Do It
• Getting off the bus or out of the car				
• Greeting adults				
• Entering school				
• Entering the classroom				
• Hanging up coat and backpack				
• Greeting classmates and adults				
• Sitting down				
• Checking calendar or schedule				
• Getting ready to work in small group				
• Getting ready to work alone				
• Waiting				
• Asking for help				
• Starting a new activity				
• Stopping an activity				
• Moving from one place to another in school				
• Getting ready for a snack				
• Having lunch				
• Finishing an activity				
• Picking up toys and materials				
• Getting ready to go home				
• Walking to the bus or car				
• Saying good-bye				
• Getting on bus or in car				

Routine Planning Form for

What
(What Routine)

_____

Cue with ☐ Visual ☐ Words _____

How
(How To Do It)

_____

_____

_____

☐ Visual ☐ Words ☐ Physical Help ☐ Gesture/Cue

Then
(Positive Reinforcement)

_____

_____

_____

☐ Visual _____ ☐ Words _____
☐ Gesture _____ ☐ Activity _____

Teaching Sequence for Routines

1. Cue with

   ❑ Visual

   ❑ Words _____

2. Get a look (joint attending).

3. Model

4. Wait

5. Watch for imitation

6. Reinforce with positive

   ❑ Visual

   ❑ Words _____

   ❑ Physical gesture _____

   ❑ Activity _____

7. Record

Target Skills for a Specific Routine

Name of Student _____

Routine _____

Required Target Skills _____

Additional Target Skills That Can Be Taught in This Routine

Social Interaction Skills _____

_____

_____

Communication Skills _____

_____

_____

Behavior Skills
(Repetitive/Stereotyped) _____

_____

_____

CHAPTER

6

Use Play To Teach Specific Skills

Professionals determine the presence of autism/PDD by observing behaviors, or the absence of behaviors, according to the criteria provided in the *Diagnostic and Statistical Manual of Mental Disorders, Fourth Edition, Text Revision (DSM–IV–TR)* of the American Psychiatric Association (2000). Because autism is a pervasive developmental disorder noticeable in early childhood, it is no surprise that many of the behavioral examples in the *DSM–IV–TR* discussion of autism/PDD criteria relate to play. Improving behaviors such as social play, spontaneous make-believe play, and imaginative play serves the important purpose of helping young children with autism/PDD function more like their typical peers and engage in typical childhood activities. These activities in turn help improve other critical skills. This chapter discusses the following:

◎ Using guidelines to teach play and to use play to teach other skills

◎ Designing play activities aimed at children with autism/PDD

◎ Developing plans that integrate specific skills into play activities

Guidelines

Using play to teach skills is a developmentally appropriate strategy. While certain play-based activities may require modifications or adaptations for the young child with autism, play is a wonderful way for parents, teachers, and caregivers to engage children and teach many skills. There is much evidence from the field of early childhood intervention that play is not only appropriate at this age, but that it is very important in the development of language and social skills. Following are some guidelines about the use of individualized play-based instruction.

Use play to promote children's overall development.

According to research, the poor play skills of young children with autism/PDD cause a negative developmental pattern: Young children with autism/PDD don't know how to play or don't play naturally (i.e., spontaneously). Because they don't know how to play or don't play naturally, children with autism/PDD don't play very often or very well. When young children with autism/PDD do not play very often or very well, the development of other specific skills may be negatively impacted. Skills in the areas of language, social interaction, and behavior may suffer when children don't learn and practice them during typical play activities. Skills such as sharing, turn taking, joint attention, requesting, participating in a pair or group activity, and verbalizing ideas are often improved during play and diminished without play.

Lilly serves as a good example of what happens when play is absent or limited in a preschooler with autism/PDD. Lilly has many strengths but she does not engage in make-believe play. Unlike some of the other children in the preschool class who play in the kitchen center, Lilly doesn't have tea parties for the dolls, has never pretended to eat the play cook-  ies with a friend, and has never agreed to be part of the "family" that takes turns setting the table, cooking, and eating. Her teacher believes that Lilly's language skills would improve if Lilly engaged in some pretend play with the other students. As it is now, Lilly often remains silent. Consequently, the other children ignore her because she won't join them in their make-believe play. This increased isolation has reduced Lilly's opportunities for socialization.

Teach children how to play.

Fortunately there is evidence of another pattern involving play: Children with autism/PDD can learn how to play. Because play often requires specific skills that children with autism/PDD lack in the areas of language, social interaction, and behavior, learning to play may be difficult for them and may require highly structured or modified situations. As the child with autism learns the process of playing and becomes comfortable with increased social interactions, however, he or she will master more skills. Teaching children with autism/PDD through play not only improves their play skills but is an excellent strategy for remediating skill deficits in language, social interaction, and behavior.

For example, we know that it is sometimes difficult to keep Caleb engaged in meaningful activities and to prevent him from self-stimulatory behaviors. Because Caleb does not seek out others for play, his mother has used a highly structured play activity with small toy cars and a ramp to teach him to attend and to follow directions. While it has not been easy, Caleb has learned to sit on the floor across from his mother and catch a car as it rolls down the ramp. Then he will put the car on top of the ramp and push it so that it rolls back toward his

mother. At first, Caleb's mother had to model the action and guide his hand to let go of his car after her verbal direction. Now Caleb watches her face and listens. When she says, "Go," he lets his car go down the ramp. His mom is thrilled that Caleb has learned to attend and to follow a verbal direction without any physical prompting. Her next step is to generalize the skill by using the same direction, "Go," before Caleb pushes a large truck to her.

Of course, the specific, discrete skills in language, social interaction and behavior that are necessary for play can also be taught by other means. However, children usually learn best when functional skills are taught in real-life situations with ample opportunities to practice. Preschoolers often learn to play more quickly if they are taught the skills required to play while they are playing.

Use play to facilitate involvement with adults and peers.

Preschoolers with autism/PDD have many characteristics in common with their same-age peers. It is important to treat them as children, not just as autistic children. Many young children, regardless of whether they have a disability, enjoy activities involving music, gross-motor actions, toy play, and games. Adults and peers will often readily and happily engage young children with autism/PDD in play because it is enjoyable and stimulating for everyone. We share common activities because we all understand and appreciate them.

For example, Rusty is an active little boy. When we design instruction for him, we want to capitalize on his interests, including his enjoyment of toy play. If we were to force Rusty to sit at a table for hours repeating isolated motor imitations, the situation would be difficult for everyone, especially Rusty. Isolated imitations might work for another child, but would not be intrinsically enjoyable for Rusty. Consequently, he probably would not repeat the actions on his own. In addition, long table sessions might result in resistance or even a tantrum, which would prevent Rusty from learning anything. Instead, we could structure a simple play activity like rolling a beach ball back and forth. This activity would involve Rusty in enjoyable play while teaching him to imitate a physical action and to take

turns. To make the activity even more effective, we could include language by modeling a verbal routine like, "Rusty's turn, Ms. Miller's turn" while he plays with the adaptive PE teacher. Because Rusty's friend Mia also likes to play with balls, she and Rusty can be paired

together in the same activity. Mia will enjoy playing with Rusty and won't have to be forced to engage with him. The teacher can encourage the children by teaching them another verbal routine, "Rusty's turn, Mia's turn."

Design play activities that meet individual needs.

To teach preschoolers with autism/PDD, it is necessary to respect their age and developmental level, as well as the severity or pervasiveness of their disability. Children's interests, attention span, activity patterns, tolerance for noise or light, preferences for shapes, colors, and textures, and other characteristics all influence teaching and learning. Consequently, we want to design teaching activities that respect the individual child. For example, we know that Caleb starts to flap his hands repeatedly when he is confused. When we design a play lesson for Caleb, we often use one that keeps his hands busy and keeps him moving. One of his favorite activities is to play with bubbles made with a hoop and detergent. Caleb loves to touch and chase the bubbles and his teacher has used a bubble

activity to teach him to imitate her as she waves the wand and blows on the bubbles. Caleb has learned to follow both directions. His teacher first taught him to imitate waving ("wave") and blowing ("blow") during one-to-one direct instruction, but Caleb tired easily during those sessions. So Caleb's teacher reduced the time spent in isolated imitation and increased the time spent playing with the bubbles. Caleb has demonstrated that he understands both directions and follows them independently. Tailoring a play activity to Caleb's needs resulted in success.

Experiment with ways to use play.

Play can teach a wide variety of skills. Last chapter, we mentioned that almost any activity can be structured and taught as a routine. Similarly, the sky is the limit when it comes to playing with young children. Almost anything a child does can be turned into a play activity and almost any skill can be incorporated into play activities, such as those listed on pages 105–106. Because preschoolers with autism/PDD often have many skills to learn, play is a perfect vehicle for teaching and learning. As we explain next how to structure play activities, we will provide some examples that show their adaptability. Do not limit your efforts to our suggestions, though. Experiment and explore the possibilities!

Specific Strategies

When used with young children with autism/PDD, most play activities will require planning a high level of structure and modifications from their typical format. This section suggests some basic strategies to use when designing play activities for young children.

Use a face-to-face physical position.

Children with autism/PDD often have problems making eye contact, attending (especially attending jointly with another person), engaging in play with others instead of alone, and joining in activities, so it is a good idea to use a face-to-face position during most play. For example, Lilly is resistant to play with others. So, when her mother wants Lilly to play, she uses a small corner area of her family room. She places Lilly on the floor with her back to the corner, spreads her own legs to provide a boundary for Lilly, and then

begins her play activities. When Lilly is seated and working in the preschool classroom, her teacher places her at a small table and sits across from her. If Lilly consistently tries to leave the table, her teacher can position the table diagonally so that Lilly is seated against a corner wall.

Use additional boundaries or people.

Some young children with autism are especially active or resistant to controlled situations in which they are required to sit or do things they do not want to do. When playing with a child who has these issues, you can create additional boundaries. In Chapter 3, we presented ideas for structuring the environment. For play activities, it may be necessary to take some of those ideas one step further. Play often excites young children and you may encounter resistance or attempted escape, especially when play requires attention and demonstration of specific skills. To prevent escape and maintain attention, try the following ideas.

Help

Ask a friend, relative, or paraprofessional to assist. Sometimes the easiest way to ensure a child's cooperation is to have an adult sit or stand behind the child and help by guiding his or her movements. This type of guidance or prompting is helpful for young children who have communication problems or who are just beginning to learn in structured situations. Remember to follow two key rules: Be gentle and use the least amount of guidance possible. The second adult's role is to help the child learn the activity, not to force compliance. For example, when Rusty learns to shake the maracas during group music and dance, the teacher stands in front of Rusty and shows him what to do. The paraprofessional stands behind him and guides him so he gets the feel of the movement. The paraprofessional does not use physical force to make Rusty imitate the teacher's actions.

Environment

Arrange the environment so that safety is ensured. We have already mentioned the idea of separating areas of the home or the classroom and designating them for specific purposes. When outdoor play is on the schedule, it is important to think ahead so that children remain safe. Some preschoolers with autism run away from situations and try to escape specific activities. For outdoor play, be sure that the area is fenced. Fencing options include clear plastic fences with hinges for flexible design in

small areas as well as more traditional wood or metal fences. Inside the classroom, make sure that the door has an alarm that beeps when it is opened, and always have an emergency plan for young students who run out of the room. Caleb often wanders, so at school the teacher has put a sign by the door with his picture and a red circle and slash (i.e., no) on top of a picture of the door. In addition, the staff has practiced what to do if Caleb starts to wander. They know exactly how to signal each other that he's leaving and they have a plan that indicates who will go after him and who will stay with the other children.

Be enthusiastic, emphatic, and directive.

Preschoolers with autism/PDD often seem to be in their own world, isolated from others around them. Attempting to engage them and maintain their attention to a play activity is challenging. It is also difficult for many teachers and parents to continue trying interactions day in and day out when the children provide little feedback and social reinforcement. Despite these challenges, it is critical for adults to project enthusiasm. Key behaviors include demonstrating exaggerated facial expressions like big smiles, using an enthusiastic voice that grabs the child's attention, and directing the child firmly when teaching and playing. One

way to improve adults' performance on these key teaching behaviors is to videotape play sessions and then review them as a team. Professionals and parents can offer feedback to each other. We recommend that interactions with young children who have autism be conducted with a rate of enthusiasm that is about two or three times greater than that with typically developing children.

Impose time limits.

When you begin any teaching sequence with a young child, you are really teaching them how to learn. Regardless of the specific skill targeted or the activity used to teach it, preschoolers must first learn what the teaching situation is all about. What do they have to do first? How long will it last? Will they have to do things they don't like? When can they stop? For a young child who has not had to sit down and participate actively in a teaching–learning situation or does not live in a structured environment, the adjustment can be difficult. Skills like sitting down, staying in one place, and listening can be very difficult for some children.

We have already discussed the importance of physical boundaries and provided suggestions that should help with sitting and staying in Chapter 3. You will also need to effectively communicate your expectations and help the child understand that activities have a starting and stopping point. Doing so should prevent long drawn-out battles with children who do not understand what they should do and how long they will have to do it. Start by imposing some structure in terms of your expectations related to time. The easiest way we know to do this is with a timer. Timers come in all shapes, sizes, and styles. Our favorite is called the TimeTimer. This timer displays a red section indicating how much time has been set. The red section gradually disappears as time elapses. While we do not recommend this product for all situations, it has a distinct advantage when used with preschoolers who have communication and behavior difficulties because it includes a visual display. You also can use auditory (beeper) timers. Regardless

of the type of timer used, it is important to use it consistently. Every time you begin a play activity, show the child the timer and then set it for a specified amount of time. When you encounter resistance in play activities, set the timer for very short periods of time (1 to 2 minutes) and stop immediately when time is up. When the timer goes off, end the activity and celebrate. With young children, this structure will pay off quickly as they learn that there is a beginning and an end to every activity. If they complete the required time, they will get to stop. Of course, you should combine the timer with a visual cue whenever possible and follow an activity the child does not like with one he or she does like. (Use the Now–Next form from Chapter 4.)

Focus on specific skills when playing.

While unstructured, unplanned, free play is sometimes appropriate for a young child who has autism/PDD, teaching a child to play or to learn play-related skills will require focus. There are many specific skills that are integral to the process, but the young child with autism/PDD may not imitate naturally or may not acquire skills unless they are emphasized and directly addressed during activities. In the next section of this chapter, we have provided a planning form that should help you as you teach. Before using the form, review the skills that are related to play and decide on a starting point for your individual child or student. The list that follows presents some key skills that can be addressed in play activities. It reflects skills that are a good match for play activities but it is not intended to be comprehensive. Feel free to add other skills you want to teach—we believe that almost anything can be taught through play. Once you have targeted a skill, plan and begin to play.

> ### Skills That Can Be Taught in Play Activities
> - Eye contact
> - Attending with body/head position
> - Joint attending
> - Sitting
> - Remaining in an area

- Listening

- Touching/Accepting touch

- Showing excitement

- Showing enjoyment

- Remaining close to another person

- Pretending/Make believe

- Turn taking

- Gross-motor skills (jumping, running, skipping, throwing)

- Fine-motor skills (picking things up, stacking, opening, closing)

- Imitating motor actions (waving, clapping, sitting)

- Imitating facial expressions (smiling, laughing, frowning)

- Imitating language

- Communicating requests/Rejecting

- Receptive-language skills, like pointing to or retrieving a specific object

- Following directions

- Matching

- Determining cause and effect

Plans for Play Activities

Plan how you will teach a preschooler with autism/PDD to play just as you plan how you will teach any other important skill. Following is a simple five-step teaching sequence to help you with your planning:

① **Show**

Show your preschooler what to do.

② **Tell**

As you are showing, tell the child with a visual or a simple, one- or two-word direction.

③ **Wait**

Give the child time to respond.

④ **Help**

If the child does not respond, help by assisting, gesturing, or modeling again.

⑤ **Celebrate**

Once the child demonstrates the skill, get excited and celebrate with smiles, hugs, cheers, claps, and whatever else works!

To help you plan using these steps, we have included a simple form at the end of this chapter, along with an example below. In our example, we have presented our plan for Lilly that focuses on turn taking during a play activity with bubbles.

Planning Your Play Activity

Name of Student _Lilly_

Target Skill _turn taking_

Specific Play Activity _bubbles_

Materials Needed _small jar of bubbles with hoop_

❶ How will you **SHOW**?
- ☑ Modeling by _teacher and asst. take turns_
- ☐ Video of _blowing bubbles_

❷ How will you **TELL**?
- ☐ Visual cue of _____
- ☐ Photo/icon/other _____
- ☑ Verbal direction to _Blow. My turn. Your turn._
  (Specific Words)

❸ How long will you **WAIT**? _30 seconds_
  (Seconds/Minutes)

❹ How will you **HELP**?
- ☑ Gesture _asst. will exaggerate movements_
  (What Movement)
- ☑ Guidance _asst. will hold hoop to Lilly's mouth_
  (Who and How)

❺ How will you **CELEBRATE**?
- ☑ Smiles   ☑ Hugs
- ☐ High-Fives   ☐ Claps
- ☑ Other _Yea Lilly!_

Consider all your options.

There are so many options for play that you will have many choices, including dance, rhymes, songs with movements, games, puppets, and toy play. The list that follows provides a number of play activities from which you can select those that are most appropriate for each individual child. We suggest you begin with the basics (i.e., simple activities that do not require a lot of equipment yet teach important foundation skills). For example, peekaboo is a game we use with Caleb to get a response from him. When he plays peekaboo, we add a tickle at the end, which makes him laugh. This game gets Caleb's attention, teaches him cause and effect, and encourages him to show excitement, all important in his continued development.

Ideas for Play

- Peekaboo
- Tickle
- So big
- Rolling a ball
- Running
- Tag
- Follow the leader
- Duck duck goose
- Red light, green light
- Hammering/pounding with spoons and pans
- Pretend with household objects (imitating mom and dad)
- Blocks, pop beads, snap toys, large LEGOs
- Cars/trucks for rolling, racing, matching colors
- Puzzles of shapes, animals, colors
- Music and movement songs
- Sandbox for digging, pouring, buckets
- Water tables
- Art activities with clay, playdough, paint
- Koosh balls
- Gel bracelets
- Goo

- Tubes with water
- Wands with sparklers
- Vibrating/mechanical toys
- Animal-sound pull toys
- Number boxes that are pushed
- Shape sorters
- Counting toys
- Play telephones

Raise your expectations.

When teaching with play activities, you should continually raise your expectations. Whether the young child with autism/PDD needs to work more independently, attend for longer periods of time, complete an activity with less assistance,  improve his tolerance for touch, or master a more complicated task, it is critical that he or she not get stuck doing the same things repeatedly. Adults must raise expectations for performance and then plan and use activities that fit those higher expectations. Always celebrate today's accomplishments, but look ahead to tomorrow's challenges.

Supporting References and Resources

American Psychiatric Association. (2000). *Diagnostic and statistical manual of mental disorders* (4th ed., Text Rev.). Washington, DC: Author.

Barry, L. M., & Burlew, S. B. (2004). Using social stories to teach choice and play skills to children with autism. *Focus on Autism and Other Developmental Disabilities, 19*(1), 45–51.

Bernard-Opitz, V., Ing, S., & Kong, T. Y. (2004). Comparison of behavioral and natural play interventions for young children with autism. *Autism: The International Journal of Research & Practice, 8*(3), 319–333.

Early Childhood Cosortium. (2002). *Play in practice: Case studies in young children's play* (C. R. Brown & C. Marchant, Eds.). St. Paul, MN: Redleaf Press.

Lantz, J. F., Nelson, J. M., & Loftin, R. L. (2004). Guiding children with autism in play: Applying the integrated play group model in group settings. *Teaching Exceptional Children, 37*(2), 8–14.

Miller, L. (1991). *Play activities for children birth to nine years.* Amherst, MA: University of Massachusetts. Retrieved December 30, 2004, from the National Network for Child Care Web site: http://www.nncc.org/Curriculum/play.activities.html

Morris, L. R., & Schulz, L. (1989). *Creative play activities for children with disabilities: A resource book for teachers and parents.* Champaign, IL: Human Kinetics.

Norris, J. (2000). *Play and learn series.* Monterey, CA: Evan-Moor Educational.

Norris, J. (2000). *Teaching young children.* Monterey, CA: Evan-Moor Educational.

Rettig, M. A., & McCarthy-Rettig, K. (2002). *Directed play: 230 activities for young children.* Longmont, CO: Sopris West.

Rogers, S. J. (1999). Intervention for young children with autism: From research to practice. *Infants and Young Children, 12*(2), 1–16.

Stahmer, A. C., Ingersoll, B., & Carter, C. (2003). Behavioral approaches to promoting play. *The International Journal of Research & Practice, 7*(4), 401–413.

Terpstra, J. E., Higgins, K., & Pierce, T. (2002). Can I play? Classroom-based interventions for teaching play skills to children with autism. *Focus on Autism and Other Developmental Disabilities, 17*(2), 119–126.

Thomas, N., & Smith, C. (2004). Developing play skills in children with autistic spectrum disorders. *Education Psychology in Practice, 20*(3), 195–206.

Whitaker, P. (2004). Fostering communication and shared play between mainstream peers and children with autism: Approaches, outcomes and experiences. *British Journal of Special Education, 31*(4), 215–222.

Whitney, T. (1998). *Kids like us: Using persona dolls in the classroom*. St. Paul, MN: Redleaf Press.

Williams, E., Reddy, V., & Costall, A. (2001). Taking a closer look at functional play in children with autism. *Journal of Autism and Developmental Disorders, 31*(1), 67–77.

CHAPTER 6 APPENDIX
Reproducible Form

Planning Your Play Activity

Name of Student _____

Target Skill _____

Specific Play Activity _____

Materials Needed _____

❶ How will you **SHOW**?

   ❑ Modeling by _____

   ❑ Video of _____

❷ How will you **TELL**?

   ❑ Visual cue of _____

   ❑ Photo/icon/other _____

   ❑ Verbal direction to _____
   (Specific Words)

❸ How long will you **WAIT**? _____
   (Seconds/Minutes)

❹ How will you **HELP**?

   ❑ Gesture _____
   (What Movement)

   ❑ Guidance _____
   (Who and How)

❺ How will you **CELEBRATE**?

   ❑ Smiles   ❑ Hugs

   ❑ High-Fives   ❑ Claps

   ❑ Other _____

CHAPTER

7

Use Individual Trials

It is important to be familiar with many different and effective teaching strategies for young children with autism/PDD. Chapters 2 through 6 discussed using visual communication techniques, structuring the environment, scheduling daily activities, establishing and teaching routines, and teaching through play activities. This chapter provides information related to another important approach to teaching young children with autism: teaching skills using individual trials. Individual trial teaching focuses on teaching specific skills one at a time in a highly structured, direct format. Each skill is taught using a consistent and systematic step-by-step teaching sequence that will be discussed in detail. In this chapter, we explain the following:

◎ Using guidelines for individual-trial teaching

◎ Selecting and defining target behaviors

◎ Using components of an individual-trial teaching sequence

◎ Employing strategies for continuous improvement

Guidelines

Because individual-trial teaching is less natural and more highly structured than using routines or play, attention should be paid to why it is used. The information in this section provides two important elements to consider and use as a guide when using individual-trial teaching.

Use individual trials to focus on specific skills.

Evidence suggests that several core skills like attending, imitating, and following directions can effectively be taught to young children with autism/PDD using an individual-trial approach. For example, Caleb's visual attention to tasks and materials has improved since his teacher began an individual-trial approach with him. Caleb now looks at items in his work area for a sustained period of time and even briefly engages in joint attention with his teacher during some activities.

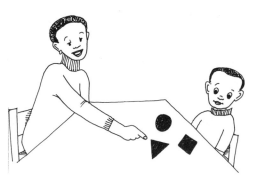

Ensure that data collection and review are consistent.

Observation and recording of data related to children's performance is possible with almost any teaching methodology. However, with other instructional approaches, observation and recording may be more complicated. When children's actions overlap or when several behaviors occur simultaneously, teachers and parents may find it difficult to determine whether a behavior occurred and whether its occurrence was exactly as required. Conversely, when teaching is carried out as individual trials, a child's performance on each individual trial can be easily observed and immediately recorded. A specific standard for a behavior can be clearly established and the child's performance measured against that standard. The data collected are vital when evaluating progress. For example, Rusty has been learning to point to an object named by his teacher. After several

weeks of teaching, she can now show Rusty two objects, say the name of one object, and ask him to point to it. He has been able to correctly identify 25 objects this way approximately 90% of the time. Rusty's teacher is excited about his improvement, which she can determine by comparing earlier trials to current ones.

Use a direct and individual approach.

When teaching young children who have autism/PDD, it is critically important to attend to the many environmental issues that impact learning. Arranging the environment to decrease distractions, providing visuals for enhanced communication, and establishing routines are all excellent ways to improve attention, increase understanding, and prevent behavior problems. Research suggests, however, that there are specific skills that may be mastered more quickly if taught directly and individually. The individual-trial model of instruction includes some steps that may not be necessary for children whose development is more typical. These steps, which include strategies like prompting and providing immediate positive reinforcement, are part of a more direct instructional style needed by many children with autism/PDD. When children do not learn incidentally, do not attend sufficiently, and do not imitate naturally, individual-trial teaching may be the most effective and efficient method to use for some skills.

It is important, though, to remember that young children with autism/PDD are still young children. Their developmental level, style of learning, tolerance for restrictions on movement, and susceptibility to fatigue must be considered. Individual-trial teaching should not be used with all children or for all skills. Care should be taken to avoid overwhelming young children with excessive demands.

As with any instructional technique, the approach should meet the child's needs without becoming overly intrusive or aversive. For example, Caleb's teacher recognizes that he is still young and becomes frustrated easily. She carefully schedules his work sessions and does not extend his direct teaching time longer than 5 minutes at a time.

Minimize potential problems.

Research related to the education of children with autism/PDD has identified several concerns related to the individual-trial teaching approach, including problems with generalization of skills, dependence on prompting, and the limited usefulness of some behaviors commonly taught this way. Teachers and parents should structure individual-trial teaching to minimize the impact of these and other problems that might arise. For example, if generalization is a problem, then several different adults should teach a particular skill in several different environments using several different items.

When Lilly was younger, her parents recognized that generalization was an issue. They used an individual-trial approach to teaching her to imitate some physical actions like clapping, waving good-bye, and blowing a kiss. Lilly began to imitate

the actions with them at home but wouldn't wave to anyone else or clap unless prompted. Fortunately, her parents saw what was happening and quickly involved Lilly's preschool teacher, grandparents, and neighbors. Soon everyone was helping Lilly practice her skills and encouraging her to use them regardless of where she was or who was with her. Lilly began to use the skills with everyone.

Target Behaviors

To teach a behavior and then determine whether a young child with autism/PDD has mastered that behavior, the teacher or parent must first target and define a specific behavior. Behaviors should be both observable and measurable and standards related to the level of independence of the action should be determined before teaching is begun. Here are some key questions to ask when determining if a target behavior is appropriately defined.

Is the behavior observable?

The first step in teaching a behavior is to describe it in observable terms. Observable behaviors are usually defined with action verbs such as *points, touches, says, looks, walks, sits, repeats, claps,* and *stands.* Behaviors that do not meet this standard include those described by adjectives (e.g., *friendly, active, caring*) or by passive verbs such as *seems to, wants to,* or *can relate to.* We often recommend to parents, teachers, and caregivers that when targeting a behavior goal, they describe the behavior on a see-and-hear chart (see example). This requires adults to specify what they would like to see or hear the child do. A blank form is provided in Appendix 7.

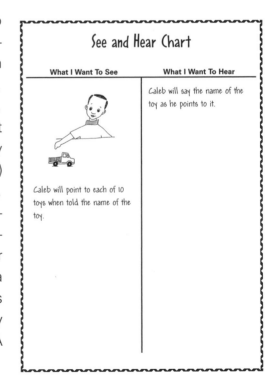

See and Hear Chart

What I Want To See	What I Want To Hear
Caleb will point to each of 10 toys when told the name of the toy.	Caleb will say the name of the toy as he points to it.

Is the behavior measurable?

Most observable behaviors will also be measurable in one of several ways. Either the behavior can be counted (when the frequency of the behavior is the issue), timed (when changing the duration of the behavior is the goal), or described (when the intensity, location, or type of behavior is important). Before beginning individual-trial teaching, decide how you will measure the child's progress and locate or develop a data recording form so you can maintain consistent records. Data collection forms should be easy to use and convenient for everyone involved in the teaching program. Later in this chapter we will discuss data recording and collection and provide several samples of forms.

Are conditions clearly explained?

Any circumstances that relate to either the child's demonstration of the behavior or the assistance provided by adults should be clear to everyone who works with the young child. Knowledge of where, when, how, and with whom the behavior occurs is critical. Specific criteria include the following conditions.

Environment

For example, if Rusty is learning to pick up his toys, should he pick them up both at school and at home?

People Involved

For example, when Caleb learns to make eye contact, does that mean looking at his peers or just attending to adults?

Assistance

For example, if Lilly can follow a verbal direction to match a blue square to another blue square, will the verbal direction be the only cue or will her teacher also point to the squares?

Timing

For example, can Rusty take his time picking up his toys or must he follow the direction within 1 minute?

Mastery Criteria

For example, when will we be satisfied that Caleb can identify his classmates by pointing to each one after hearing a name? Does he need to be correct 100% or 80% of the time? Criteria should relate directly to the behaviors as they were defined and can be a number or percent of occurrences (Rusty only tantrums once a day now), a duration (Rusty only tantrums for 5 minutes now), or a specific quality (Rusty's tantrums no longer include spitting).

There are many conditions related to behavior and it is impossible to list them all here. However, it is important to describe the targeted behavior as completely as possible, so that when data are recorded they will be accurate and reflect consistent expectations.

Are the skills appropriate and necessary?

With young children who have autism/PDD, it can be difficult to know which skills are most important, which skills are prerequisites for other skills and so should be taught first, and which skills are critical for functioning in typical, non-restrictive environments. Although there are no simple answers to these questions and each child's individual needs will be the basis for all decisions related to instruction, we do recognize that families and teachers often benefit from expert advice. Numerous identification and assessment instruments are available that list specific skills related to childhood development or characteristics of autism. In the Resources section at the end of this chapter, we have provided a list of those instruments.

Beginning Curriculum Guide

Attending Skills
1. Sits in a chair independently
2. Makes eye contact in response to name
3. Makes eye contact when given the instruction "Look at me"
4. Responds to the direction "Hands down"

Imitation Skills
1. Imitates gross motor movements
2. Imitates actions with objects
3. Imitates fine motor movements
4. Imitates oral motor movements

Receptive Language Skills
1. Follows one-step instructions
2. Identifies body parts
3. Identifies objects
4. Identifies pictures
5. Identifies familiar people
6. Follows verb instructions
7. Identifies verbs in pictures
8. Identifies objects in the environment
9. Points to pictures in a book
10. Identifies objects by function
11. Identifies possession
12. Identifies environmental sounds

Expressive Language Skills
1. Points to desired items in response to "What do you want?"
2. Points to desired items spontaneously
3. Imitates sounds and words
4. Labels objects
5. Labels pictures
6. Verbally requests desired items

7. States or gestures yes and no for preferred and nonpreferred items
8. Labels familiar people
9. Makes a choice
10. Reciprocates greetings
11. Answers social questions
12. Labels verbs in pictures, others, and self
13. Labels objects by function
14. Labels possession

Pre-academic Skills
1. Matches
   - Identical objects
   - Identical pictures
   - Objects to pictures
   - Pictures to objects
   - Colors, shapes, letters, numbers
   - Nonidentical objects
   - Objects by association
2. Completes simple activities independently
3. Identifies colors
4. Identifies shapes
5. Identifies letters
6. Identifies numbers
7. Counts by rote to 10
8. Counts objects

Self-help Skills
1. Drinks from a cup
2. Uses fork and spoon when eating
3. Removes shoes
4. Removes socks
5. Removes pants
6. Removes shirt
7. Uses napkin/tissue
8. Is toilet-trained for urination

Note. From *Behavioral Intervention for Young Children with Autism: A Manual for Parents and Professionals* (p. 66), by C. M. Maurice with G. Green and S. C. Luce, 1996, Austin, TX: PRO-ED, Inc. Copyright 1996 by PRO-ED, Inc. Reprinted with permission.

In addition to the assessment instruments, the Resources section also lists two sources of information that may provide guidance in determining which skills to teach a young child with autism/PDD. While we do not endorse a specific product, we believe readers will find these helpful. One source is the Beginning Curriculum Guide on page 66 of *Behavioral Intervention for Young Children with Autism,* edited by Catherine Maurice. This curriculum guide is included in a chapter by Taylor and McDonough that discusses teaching programs. The simple one-page list of skills may be helpful for teachers and parents, especially when using an individual-trial format.

Kathleen Quill has included an Assessment of Social and Communication Skills for Children with Autism in her book *Do-Watch-Listen-Say*. The assessment, which has recently been published as a separate product, includes three checklists related to core skills, social skills, and communication skills. These checklists help teachers and parents determine which skills to teach, the order in which to teach them, and how a child is doing on a specific skill.

Before the teaching of any skill is begun, though, the individual child's strengths, challenges, and related issues, and the family needs should be thoroughly reviewed and discussed. Guides and assessments can be useful but should never replace common sense and a complete individual assessment. Moreover, we do not recommend the exclusive use of individual-trial teaching for young children with autism/PDD. While individual-trial teaching is effective with some skills and some children, it is often inappropriate or ineffective when teaching specific communication, social, and behavioral skills.

Components

Individual-trial teaching is an approach based on the principles of applied behavior analysis. Instruction follows clear and specific steps that reflect basic behavioral principles. For maximum effectiveness, involved adults should all become familiar with the components of an individual trial and then use the approach consistently. Following are the components generally included in individual-trial teaching.

Use short, clearly communicated work sessions.

To begin the process of individual-trial teaching, you will first need to establish times and places for work sessions and teach the young child what to expect. Deciding on the length of time a preschooler can work at a task is tricky. Start with very short sessions of 2 to 3 minutes and gradually increase the amount of time by 1 or 2 minutes as the child's tolerance increases. Eventually you may be able to structure 7- to 10-minute sessions. To minimize resistance, use a verbal cue and a visual cue when directing the child to the teaching area. A visual cue, either by showing an object or a representation of one, is an excellent signal to young children that the teaching sequence is about to begin. There are numerous pictures, icons, and photographs that can be used to indicate an individual-trial work session. A picture of the work area, an icon that shows the toys or materials used in the session, or a photograph of the young child at work are all appropriate visuals. If you consistently pair your verbal and visual directions and

then begin to work immediately, you will teach the young child with autism/PDD that as soon as he or she sees the visual, work is about to begin. For children whose receptive language skills are poor or whose temperament is stubborn, visuals should improve their understanding and lessen behavioral resistance to tasks.

Likewise, at the end of an individual-trial session, a consistent verbal cue like "Finished," or "Work over," can signal the completion of the work session. Pairing the verbal cue with another visual or an American Sign Language sign should communicate the end of work even more clearly. Finally, you might want to use the Now–Next card mentioned in Chapter 4. A visual on the second half of the card that indicates a preferred play activity reminds a child that after work comes play.

Use a structured setting.

We have already discussed the need for a variety of settings when working with young children who have autism/PDD. Chapter 3, which addressed structuring the environment, and Chapter 6, on play, both provide suggestions for arranging spaces for instruction. For individual-trial teaching, many of the same considerations are important. Because individual-trial teaching is a direct rather than incidental or unstructured teaching strategy, a location that allows for face-to-face or side-by-side instruction is necessary. In most cases, a young child should be seated directly in front of the teacher or parent, either on the floor or at a table. The instructional space should be free of visual and auditory distractions and have boundaries to encourage the child to stay in the space. Toys or other materials should be readily available but kept out of sight until needed. Any materials used for observation or data collection should be out of reach of the child but convenient to the adult. It is best to have a second adult available to observe and record information, though we know that this is not always possible or practical.

The general rule for establishing instructional space for individual-trial teaching is to keep it simple, uncluttered, and distraction free.

Make sure trials have a beginning and an end.

One of the keys to an individual-trial approach is ensuring that there really are individual trials. This means that you begin a teaching sequence in a consistent manner and that you end it in a consistent manner. In between each trial, there should be a brief time interval that serves to differentiate one trial from another. Teachers and parents can indicate the beginning and end of trials in several ways, including by verbal direction and by visual cues and modeling.

Verbal Direction

Verbal cues to begin an individual teaching trial should be short and emphatic, but not harsh. Typically, adults will use a standard phrase like, "Ready?" or the child's name with a direction, like, "Caleb, touch...." Almost any word or two- or three-word phrase will work as a signal to begin a trial. Consistency is key. The same word or phrase should be used every time you begin the trial. In this way, the young child with autism/PDD will learn to associate the verbal direction with the activity. As the word and the behavior become paired, the child should start to understand that the signal means it is time to demonstrate the behavior. Understanding the process should help reduce resistance.

Visual Cues and Modeling

We have discussed the importance of using visuals to improve the ability of young children with autism/PDD to understand what is being said to them. Because individual-trial teaching is demanding and may be a challenging style for some children to accept, it is even more important to integrate the use of visuals into this methodology. Just as visuals can be used to indicate the beginning and end of a work session, so too can they assist with an explanation of what is expected. Showing a young child a picture of the targeted behavior, using an icon to help with the explanation, and then modeling for the child increase understanding and provide valuable cues as the child learns a new skill. Modeling can also include the child's peers who have already mastered a target behavior. For example, because Lilly already knows how to hold a book and turn the pages, she can model the skill for Caleb, who is still learning.

Use time intervals to delineate trials.

Because one of the key principles in individual-trial teaching is the "individual" part of the system, it is important to separate the trials. This separation ensures accurate record keeping and helps adults maintain a consistent teaching approach. It is not necessary to use a timer between trials, however, because the

down time should not be long. A few seconds is sufficient and the interval can be determined by counting, "One one thousand, two one thousand, three one thousand," and then beginning the next trial.

Follow these steps in the teaching trial.

There are four basic steps in an individual-trial teaching sequence:

①   Give a direction or make a request (in behavioral terms, the stimulus).

②   Wait for and then observe the child's behavior (the response).

③a Provide a positive consequence if the child's behavior meets the standard for performance (positive reinforcement).

    or

③b Prompt the child to demonstrate the behavior again if his or her performance was not correct, then provide the positive consequence.

④   Repeat over time until the criteria for mastery have been met.

The steps for each trial are also provided on the Teaching Cue Card in Appendix 7. This teaching model is the basis for individual-trial teaching and relies heavily on the power of positive reinforcement to change behavior. When a young child with autism demonstrates the correct behavior and receives social, verbal, or tangible consequences that he or she desires, the targeted behavior is rewarded and should be strengthened. Appendix 7 provides an extensive list of activities and items (List of Reinforcers) that most young children find appealing. Adults should select a wide array of positive reinforcers and then offer a limited number (two to start) of choices, recording what the child prefers because the preferences of many young children with autism are inconsistent and difficult to predict. Teachers and parents can also select some of the reinforcers from the list provided, put them on the Reinforcer Checklist in the Appendix, and ask other involved adults to select those they think will be most desired by the child. Soon a pattern will emerge, and adults will be able to determine which reinforcers are most desirable and powerful. These can be recorded on the All-Time Favorites list, also found in the Appendix.

```
╔══════════════════════════════════╗
║          All-Time Favorites        ║
║                                    ║
║  Student's Name _____  Today's Date _____ ║
║  Rater's Name _____           ║
║                                    ║
║  Write the student's six favorite reinforcers (type or specific brand). ║
║                                    ║
║   ❶ _____  ║
║                                    ║
║   ❷ _____  ║
║                                    ║
║   ❸ _____  ║
║                                    ║
║   ❹ _____  ║
║                                    ║
║   ❺ _____  ║
║                                    ║
║   ❻ _____  ║
║                                    ║
╚══════════════════════════════════╝
```

Continuous Improvement Strategies

The teaching sequence presented above is the foundation for all individual-trial teaching. However, some additional procedures can increase the chances for success with this type of instruction. We will briefly describe several of these supplementary ideas.

Record, summarize, review, and plan from data.

Because one of the hallmarks of individual-trial teaching is its reliance on recorded data, we suggest that you find tools that are easy to use and understand. At the end of this chapter are several forms to help you get started. But recording data is not the only step; the information gathered must be summarized regularly, reviewed by everyone involved, and then used as the basis for making instructional decisions. We have provided the following tools in the Appendix for this chapter.

Frequency Chart

To use the Frequency Chart, first write each target behavior and its level of prompting. Prompting can be done with a verbal direction, a visual cue, a gesture, or a physical prompt and will be discussed again in the next section. After each individual trial, put a slash on a number if the child responded correctly, beginning with the number 1 and ending with the number 5. At the end of five trials, circle the top number that has a slash. For example, when teaching Lilly to match squares, we will use five trials per session. If Lilly matches the squares correctly the first time we ask her, we put a slash mark on the 1. We do the same each time she responds correctly. At the end of five trials, we know how well she has done by counting the slash marks. In the example chart shown, she has matched correctly four of five times, or 80% of the time. By repeating the teaching process consistently and recording Lilly's performance each time, Lilly's teacher and parents can easily get a snapshot of her progress by looking at the circled numbers representing the number of correct responses per trial.

Frequency Chart

Student's Name Lilly

Write each target behavior and prompt level. After each trial, put a slash on a number if the student responds correctly, beginning with the number 1. At the end of five trials, circle the top number that has a slash.

Target Behavior	1	2	3	4	5	6	7	8	9	10
	Daily Lesson Sets									
Matching Shapes Prompt Level gesture (adult points)	5 (4) 3 2 1	5 4 3 2 1	5 4 3 2 1	5 4 3 2 1	5 4 3 2 1	5 4 3 2 1	5 4 3 2 1	5 4 3 2 1	5 4 3 2 1	5 4 3 2 1
______ Prompt Level ______	5 4 3 2 1	5 4 3 2 1	5 4 3 2 1	5 4 3 2 1	5 4 3 2 1	5 4 3 2 1	5 4 3 2 1	5 4 3 2 1	5 4 3 2 1	5 4 3 2 1
______ Prompt Level ______	5 4 3 2 1	5 4 3 2 1	5 4 3 2 1	5 4 3 2 1	5 4 3 2 1	5 4 3 2 1	5 4 3 2 1	5 4 3 2 1	5 4 3 2 1	5 4 3 2 1
______ Prompt Level ______	5 4 3 2 1	5 4 3 2 1	5 4 3 2 1	5 4 3 2 1	5 4 3 2 1	5 4 3 2 1	5 4 3 2 1	5 4 3 2 1	5 4 3 2 1	5 4 3 2 1
______ Prompt Level ______	5 4 3 2 1	5 4 3 2 1	5 4 3 2 1	5 4 3 2 1	5 4 3 2 1	5 4 3 2 1	5 4 3 2 1	5 4 3 2 1	5 4 3 2 1	5 4 3 2 1

Duration Chart

The Duration Chart should be used when recording how long a specific behavior lasts. The chart is easy to use and self-explanatory. Each time the target behavior begins, record the start time; when the behavior ends, record the stop time. Subtract

the start time from the stop time and write down the total time the child engaged in the behavior. After five sessions, compute an average by dividing the total time by five. You can then compare the beginning average to the current average to determine if the child is making sufficient progress. For example, because we want Caleb to make eye contact with peers, we record this during small-group play. We observe Caleb for 5 minutes, and after several observations, we have a good idea of whether he is using the skill independently, without prompting.

Descriptive Behavior Chart

Sometimes we are more concerned with the quality or severity of a behavior than how often or how long it occurs. This type of information usually requires more writing or structured observation during which the observer codes behaviors as they occur. To keep this process simple, we use a chart. After filling in the behavior at the top of the Descriptive Behavior Chart and its descriptors horizontally on the chart, adults can

Duration Chart

Name: Caleb Date: Oct. 3

Behavior: making eye contact with peers

Trials		Min	:	Sec
1	Stop Time	10	:	15
	Start Time	10	:	10
	Duration		:	5
2	Stop Time	10	:	24
	Start Time	10	:	18
	Duration		:	6
3	Stop Time	2	:	05
	Start Time	2	:	00
	Duration		:	5
4	Stop Time	2	:	20
	Start Time	2	:	10
	Duration		:	10
5	Stop Time	2	:	30
	Start Time	2	:	21
	Duration		:	9
	Average Duration		:	7

Descriptive Behavior Chart

Name: Rusty

Behavior: Tantrum

Date	Screams	Bites	Hits	Spits	Throws	
9/5	X	X		X	X	
9/7	X	X		X		
9/12	X		X		X	
9/13	X		X			
9/14	X		X			
9/18	X		X			

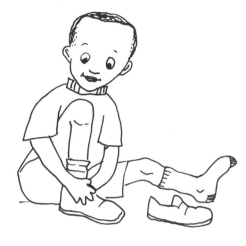

Descriptive Behavior Chart

Name: Caleb

Behavior: Shoes and Socks

Date	foot into sock	pull up sock	foot into shoe	Velcro strap			
9/5	X	X					
9/7	X	X	X				
9/12	X						
9/13	X	X	X				
9/14	X	X	X	X			
9/18	X	X	X	X			

check off the descriptors they observe instead of taking time to write the description in sentence or paragraph form. For example, Rusty's teacher has worked hard at teaching him alternatives to a tantrum when he does not get his own way. His teacher wrote the tantrum descriptors, such as spitting and hitting, on the chart. After several days of observing Rusty's tantrums and recording Rusty's actions, the teacher can see that Rusty is making progress. While he has not totally stopped tantrumming, he has stopped biting, spitting, and throwing things and now he "only" screams and hits.

When teaching positive behaviors, not behaviors that should be reduced, the same process is used. Fill in the blank chart to describe the quality of behavior desired. For example, Caleb's mother wants him to put on his shoes and socks. The chart used to record this behavior includes the steps in the process: Puts foot into sock, pulls up sock, puts foot into shoe, puts Velcro strap across top of shoe.

Address the level of prompting.

We briefly mentioned above that there are several levels of assistance or prompting that can be used during individual-trial teaching. Verbal directions or reminders, visual cues, gestures and signals, and physical guidance are all options when helping a young child learn how to perform new behaviors. However, it is critical that the type and level of prompting be addressed before teaching is begun. Decisions must be made about how to prompt, what the prompt looks like, how long the wait time will be before using a prompt, and when the prompts will be discontinued. One of the most common problems with an individual-trial teaching approach is that many adults prompt too much for too long. Any physical prompts should be as unobtrusive as possible. Prompting should be gentle guidance, not force. Adults should model prompting for each other, agree on how it will be used, and then review its use regularly. Children are unlikely to learn independent behaviors when they are consistently and frequently overprompted. Gradually and systematically reduce the level of prompting to ensure independent mastery of skills.

Start with basics and gradually raise your expectations.

One of the keys to teaching any young child is to start with basic skills and then build on them. Lilly's progress in learning to take turns is a good example of this. Her teacher first taught her to roll a large ball back and forth two times in a row while she and her teacher sat across from each other on the floor. Lilly's teacher eventually increased the turns to four, then six, then eight. Lilly now takes turns rolling the ball as many as 10 times in one play session. Her teacher has already added a smaller, new toy to the teaching situation, a truck, to help Lilly learn to  take turns with a variety of toys. Next, Lilly's teacher plans to add Lilly's friend Rosa into the activity to make sure that Lilly takes turns with her peers, not just with adults.

Lilly's progress occurred in small steps, but her teacher recognized an important concept inherent in individual-trial teaching: It is possible to make significant progress one skill at a time. By identifying key skills, teaching them to mastery, and gradually adding higher level skills, young children with autism/PDD can learn skills to help them function independently and successfully. This method is only one of many approaches but we believe that it has a place in any program for young children with autism/PDD.

Supporting References and Resources

Duker, P., Didden, R., & Sigafoos, J. (2004). *One-to-one training: Instructional procedures for learners with developmental disabilities.* Austin, TX: PRO-ED.

Kimball, J. W. (2002). Behavior-analytic instruction for children with autism: Philosophy matters. *Focus on Autism and Other Developmental Disabilities, 17*(2), 66–75.

Lovaas, O. I. (2003). *Teaching individuals with developmental delays.* Austin, TX: PRO-ED.

Maurice, C., Green, G., & Foxx, R. M. (2001). *Making a difference: Behavioral intervention for autism.* Austin, TX : PRO-ED.

Maurice, C., Green, G., & Luce, S. C. (1996). *Behavioral intervention for young children with autism: A manual for parents and professionals.* Austin, TX : PRO-ED.

Quill, K. A. (2000). *Do-watch-listen-say: Social and communication intervention for children with autism.* Baltimore: Brookes.

Romanczyk, R. G., Lockshin, S. B., & Matey, L. (2000). The children's unit for treatment and evaluation. In J. S. Handleman & S. L. Harris (Eds.), *Preschool education programs for children with autism* (2nd ed., pp. 49–94). Austin, TX: PRO-ED.

Smith, T. (2001). Discrete trial training in the treatment of autism. *Focus on Autism and Other Developmental Disabilities, 16*(2), 86–92.

Assessment Tools

Krug, D. A., Arick, J. R., & Almond, P. J. (1993). *Autism Screening Instrument for Educational Planning* (2nd ed.). Austin, TX: PRO-ED.

Lord, C., Rutter, M., DiLavore, P. C., & Risi, S. (2002). *Autism Diagnostic Observation Schedule.* Los Angeles: Western Psychological Services.

Rutter, M., LeCouteur, A., & Lord, C. (2004). *Autism Diagnostic Interview, Revised.* Los Angeles: Western Psychological Services.

Schopler, E., Lansing, M. D., & Marcus, L. M. (2005). *The Psychoeducational Profile* (3rd ed.). Austin, TX: PRO-ED.

Schopler, E., Reichler, R. J., & Reneer, B. R. (1988). *Childhood Autism Rating Scale.* Los Angeles: Western Psychological Services.

Sparrow, S. S., & Cicchetti, D. V. (2004). *Vineland Adaptive Behavior Scales* (2nd ed.). Circle Pines, MN: AGS.

CHAPTER 7 APPENDIX
Reproducible Forms

See and Hear Chart

What I Want To See   **What I Want To Hear**

Teaching Cue Card

(Individual-Trial Teaching)

1 Give the Direction or Make a Request

2 Wait and Observe

3a Reinforce

or

3b Prompt

4 Repeat

List of Reinforcers

Never leave a young child unattended when playing with edible or material reinforcers. To determine if a material reinforcer is potentially dangerous because of its size, place it in a no-choke testing tube (available form the U.S. Consumer Product Safety Comminssion at 781/364-3100) or a toilet paper tube without compressing it. If it fits entirely within the tube, in any orientation, it should not be given to children under the age of 3 or older children who still put things in their mouths.

Student's Name _____   Today's Date _____

Rater's Name _____

Does the child like _____?

Edible Reinforcers		Yes	No			Yes	No
Cereals	1. Cheerios	❏	❏	Others	28. Graham Crackers	❏	❏
	2. Fruit Loops	❏	❏		29. Animal Crackers	❏	❏
	3. Trix	❏	❏		30. Crackers	❏	❏
	4. _____	❏	❏		31. Pretzels	❏	❏
Fruit	5. Apples	❏	❏		32. Chips	❏	❏
	6. Oranges	❏	❏		33. Cheese Snacks	❏	❏
	7. Bananas	❏	❏		34. Doritos	❏	❏
	8. _____	❏	❏		35. Cookies	❏	❏
Liquids	9. Milk	❏	❏		36. Vegetables with Dip	❏	❏
	10. Chocolate Milk	❏	❏		37. _____	❏	❏
	11. Juice	❏	❏	**Material Reinforcers**			
	12. Soda Pop	❏	❏		1. Hand Cream	❏	❏
	13. Lemonade	❏	❏		2. Bubbles	❏	❏
	14. _____	❏	❏		3. Stickers	❏	❏
Frozen	15. Popsicle	❏	❏		4. Playdough	❏	❏
	16. Ice Cream	❏	❏		5. Toy Instruments	❏	❏
	17. _____	❏	❏		6. Puzzles	❏	❏
Soft	18. Pudding	❏	❏		7. Stamps and Pads	❏	❏
	19. Jell-o	❏	❏		8. Masks	❏	❏
	20. Yogurt	❏	❏		9. Crayons	❏	❏
	21. Marshmallows	❏	❏		10. Fans	❏	❏
	22. Cheese	❏	❏		11. Beanbags	❏	❏
	23. Cottage Cheese	❏	❏		12. Hats	❏	❏
	24. Peanut Butter	❏	❏		13. Mirrors	❏	❏
	25. Jam/Jelly	❏	❏		14. Books	❏	❏
	26. Applesauce	❏	❏		15. Coloring Books	❏	❏
	27. _____	❏	❏		16. Washable Markers	❏	❏
					17. Blocks	❏	❏

Page 1

	Yes	No		Yes	No
18. Paints	❏	❏	34. Climbing	❏	❏
19. Colored Chalk	❏	❏	35. Cutting Pictures	❏	❏
20. _____	❏	❏	36. Treasure Hunt	❏	❏

Activity Reinforcers

	Yes	No		Yes	No
			37. Looking at Pictures	❏	❏
1. Rocking	❏	❏	38. Basketball	❏	❏
2. Brushing Hair	❏	❏	39. Finger Paint		
3. Clapping Hands	❏	❏	with Pudding	❏	❏
4. Piggyback Rides	❏	❏	with Whipped Cream	❏	❏
5. Drawing Pictures	❏	❏	with Soap	❏	❏
6. Run Outside	❏	❏	with Paint	❏	❏
7. Hide-and-Seek	❏	❏	40. Racing	❏	❏
8. Chase	❏	❏	41. Wagon Rides	❏	❏
9. Peekaboo	❏	❏	42. Water Plants	❏	❏
10. Sing Songs	❏	❏	43. Make Treats	❏	❏
11. Sprinkle Glitter	❏	❏	44. Play with Zippers	❏	❏
12. Tickles	❏	❏	45. Blow Bubbles	❏	❏
13. Water Play	❏	❏	46. Swimming	❏	❏
14. Puppets	❏	❏	47. Listen to Music	❏	❏
15. Sand Play	❏	❏	48. Play with Typewriter	❏	❏
16. Trampoline	❏	❏	49. Turn Water On/Off	❏	❏
17. Dancing	❏	❏	50. Smell Spices	❏	❏
18. Bring Toy from Home	❏	❏	51. Surprise Box	❏	❏
19. Turn Lights On/Off	❏	❏	52. Fishing Game	❏	❏
20. Pour Liquids	❏	❏	53. Go for Walks	❏	❏
21. Videotapes	❏	❏	54. _____	❏	❏
22. Stories	❏	❏	**Social Reinforcers**		
23. Talking on the Phone	❏	❏	1. Hugs	❏	❏
24. Drawing	❏	❏	2. Shaking Hands	❏	❏
25. Draw on Chalkboard	❏	❏	3. Kisses	❏	❏
26. Lunch/Snack Helper	❏	❏	4. Tickling	❏	❏
27. Field Trips	❏	❏	5. Winking	❏	❏
28. Taking Pictures	❏	❏	6. Give Me Five	❏	❏
29. Rolling Down Hill	❏	❏	7. Smiling	❏	❏
30. Making Pictures			8. Whistling	❏	❏
with Large Noodles	❏	❏	9. Patting	❏	❏
with String	❏	❏	10. Praising	❏	❏
31. Running Errands	❏	❏	11. Back Scratch/Rub	❏	❏
32. Playing in Boxes	❏	❏	12. Praise	❏	❏
33. Dressing Up	❏	❏	13. _____	❏	❏

Reinforcer Checklist

Student's Name _____ Today's Date _____

Rater's Name _____

Check all of the reinforcers that the student likes (write in the specific brand, type, or person's name in the second column). Circle the three reinforcers that are the student's favorites.

Food   **Brand Name or Type**

❑ Cereal   _____

❑ Fruit   _____

❑ Snacks   _____

❑ Cookies   _____

❑ Crackers   _____

❑ _____   _____

❑ _____   _____

Objects   **Brand Name or Type**

❑ Magazines   _____

❑ Pictures   _____

❑ Toys   _____

❑ Manipulatives   _____

❑ _____   _____

❑ _____   _____

Social Contact   **Person's Name**

❑ Talking   _____

❑ Friends   _____

❑ Staff   _____

❑ Peers   _____

❑ _____   _____

❑ _____   _____

Activities

	Type
❑ Watching sports	_____
❑ Dancing	_____
❑ Working out	_____
❑ Other exercise	_____
❑ Games	_____
❑ Movies	_____
❑ Sewing	_____
❑ Making something	_____
❑ Drawing	_____
❑ Writing	_____
❑ Watering plants	_____
❑ Caring for animals	_____
❑ _____	_____
❑ _____	_____

Other

	Brand Name or Type
❑ Audiocassettes	_____
❑ Videos	_____
❑ Noise makers	_____
❑ Radio	_____
❑ _____	_____
❑ _____	_____

All-Time Favorites

Student's Name _____   Today's Date _____

Rater's Name _____

Write the student's six favorite reinforcers (type or specific brand).

❶ _____

❷ _____

❸ _____

❹ _____

❺ _____

❻ _____

Frequency Chart

Student's Name _____

Write each target behavior and prompt level. After each trial, put a slash on a number if the student responds correctly, beginning with the number 1. At the end of five trials, circle the top number that has a slash.

Target Behavior	Daily Lesson Sets									
	1	**2**	**3**	**4**	**5**	**6**	**7**	**8**	**9**	**10**
_____	5	5	5	5	5	5	5	5	5	5
	4	4	4	4	4	4	4	4	4	4
	3	3	3	3	3	3	3	3	3	3
Prompt Level _____	2	2	2	2	2	2	2	2	2	2
	1	1	1	1	1	1	1	1	1	1
_____	5	5	5	5	5	5	5	5	5	5
	4	4	4	4	4	4	4	4	4	4
	3	3	3	3	3	3	3	3	3	3
Prompt Level _____	2	2	2	2	2	2	2	2	2	2
	1	1	1	1	1	1	1	1	1	1
_____	5	5	5	5	5	5	5	5	5	5
	4	4	4	4	4	4	4	4	4	4
	3	3	3	3	3	3	3	3	3	3
Prompt Level _____	2	2	2	2	2	2	2	2	2	2
	1	1	1	1	1	1	1	1	1	1
_____	5	5	5	5	5	5	5	5	5	5
	4	4	4	4	4	4	4	4	4	4
	3	3	3	3	3	3	3	3	3	3
Prompt Level _____	2	2	2	2	2	2	2	2	2	2
	1	1	1	1	1	1	1	1	1	1
_____	5	5	5	5	5	5	5	5	5	5
	4	4	4	4	4	4	4	4	4	4
	3	3	3	3	3	3	3	3	3	3
Prompt Level _____	2	2	2	2	2	2	2	2	2	2
	1	1	1	1	1	1	1	1	1	1

Duration Chart

Name: _____. Date: _____

Behavior: _____

Trials _____

1	**Stop Time**	_____ : _____	
	Start Time	_____ : _____	
	Duration	_____ : _____	
2	**Stop Time**	_____ : _____	
	Start Time	_____ : _____	
	Duration	_____ : _____	
3	**Stop Time**	_____ : _____	
	Start Time	_____ : _____	
	Duration	_____ : _____	
4	**Stop Time**	_____ : _____	
	Start Time	_____ : _____	
	Duration	_____ : _____	
5	**Stop Time**	_____ : _____	
	Start Time	_____ : _____	
	Duration	_____ : _____	

Average Duration _____ : _____

Descriptive Behavior Chart

Name _____

Behavior _____

Date						

8 Teach and Improve Behavior

If you have read the other chapters in this manual, you already know how to teach many behaviors by using a variety of strategies. Because skills learned by young children are often interrelated, it makes sense that behavior can be positively impacted when young children learn new, functional skills in the areas of communication, socialization, play, and more. In fact, teaching developmentally appropriate skills in these areas is often the best way to prevent behavior problems. For that reason, behavioral issues should be approached instructionally first and addressed as a behavior management issue only when necessary. Use a positive, proactive approach that emphasizes teaching behavior rather than responding to behavior. Despite everyone's best efforts at instruction, however, sometimes a response to misbehavior is required.

This chapter provides information that will help teachers, parents, and caregivers improve overall behavior of young children with autism/PDD either by increasing specific desirable behaviors or by decreasing specific undesirable behaviors. Suggestions for creating and maintaining a positive support system for behavior include:

- Following three basic guidelines for improving behavior

- Using positive reinforcement to teach self-control

- Teaching replacement behaviors

Guidelines

To teach behavior effectively, follow three basic guidelines: (a) Directly teach desired behaviors, (b) determine the relationship between communication skills and behaviors, and (c) teach transition skills.

Teach desired behaviors directly.

Often young children with autism/PDD are not "tuned in" to others, so they may not learn positive behaviors incidentally. One of the characteristics of autistic disorder is a lack of social engagement and reciprocity. This obliviousness to others often creates a learning problem for young children who have autism/PDD. They may not observe others carefully, connect actions and their purpose, understand the feelings conveyed by their peers or by adults, or modify their behavior based on what others say and do. Because of this lack of social connectedness, many desired, positive behaviors must be directly taught. When adults understand that many behaviors are the result of an inefficient learning style, then it is clear where and how to start improving those behaviors: through systematic teaching. We have already mentioned Caleb's difficulties in tuning in and learning skills incidentally. When we teach Caleb a new behavior like sharing toys instead of grabbing toys from others, we will first use instruction—teaching Caleb to share.

Investigate the relationship between commmunication and behavior.

For many years, both professionals and parents have agreed that behavior is a tool for communication. When communication skills are impaired, the only way

to communicate feelings, needs, wants, or ideas may be through overt behavior. A young child with autism/PDD who does not understand a verbal direction, but cannot ask for help, may lie down on the floor, leave the area, or find something else to do. The child who is bothered by noise but cannot tell anyone what is wrong may scream, hold his or her ears, or run from the room. The list of possible misbehaviors related to communication is endless and may range from mild to serious. Adults should investigate the relationship between communication and a child's misbehavior, and then approach any problematic situations in a proactive, problem-solving mode.

For example, Lilly's parents know that when she has not slept and is overtired, she does not tell them in words; she cries easily and is impossible to comfort or console. Adults who work with Lilly always consider her feelings or physical problems like lack of sleep, problems that Lilly cannot communicate to them.

Teach transition skills.

The stereotypical, rigid behavior patterns common to autism can result in children having difficulties with change, particularly in transitioning from one activity, location, or person to another. Sometimes, when children are familiar and comfortable with a particular schedule, specific individuals, or even preferred toys and materials, a disruption in any of those patterns can be a challenge. Whether transition problems are due to poor communication skills, difficulty dealing with unfamiliar stimuli, or a fear of unknown or lesser known situations

is difficult to know. However, we do know that difficulty with transitions is common among young children with autism/PDD. Rusty has always enjoyed outdoor play and disliked coming inside, so when he began his preschool program, his mother made sure that his teacher was aware of this issue and planned ahead to teach him to transition into the classroom after recess. In this way, they were able to avoid a serious behavior problem.

Adults who work with young children who have autism/PDD should consider the importance of transitions and changes, plan for each individual child's transition issues, and then establish procedures that prevent problems. If behavior problems do arise, adults should investigate the child's schedule, the amount of structure in the situation, and possible strategies for dealing with unexpected variations. It is also good common sense to expect that some behavior problems will probably occur when changes occur. We must teach the child methods of dealing effectively with unexpected changes.

In an earlier chapter, we discussed Caleb's problems related to changes in personnel at school. His team has worked hard to minimize those transition-related problems and Caleb's behavior has improved significantly because of their efforts. They not only improved their communication with Caleb when changes were about to occur, but they also taught him some ways to handle the changes without falling apart. He has learned to acknowledge variations in his visual schedule and use his choice of calming activities when a new adult replaces a more familiar one in his world.

Positive Reinforcement for Self-Control

A comprehensive, positive approach to behavior is the best course for young children with autism/PDD. Strategies for teaching new skills in positive ways are provided throughout this manual. Teaching new, desirable behaviors is almost always the key to children's success. We will start by focusing on a behavior that is difficult to learn—self-control. When children engage in behaviors that are seriously disruptive, antisocial, aggressive, or even dangerous, they usually receive a negative reaction, like a reprimand ("Stop that"), punishment ("Go to your room"), or exclusion from activities ("Now we're not going to McDonald's"). While these consequences may be effective with some children when they are used consistently, often they do not work. The lack of effectiveness of punishment and other negative consequences can be due to one or several variables:

- They are not immediate.
- They are too severe or too mild.
- They are not meaningful to the child.
- They are not used consistently.
- They are not understood by the child.
- They meet the child's needs (e.g., for attention).

We offer an alternative: a positive approach to reducing unwanted, challenging behaviors. Choosing not to do something that you really want to do and demonstrating self-control are challenging, high-level competencies. If parents and professionals teach young children with autism/PDD to control their most problematic, undesirable behaviors, then those children will reap many benefits. For example, they can be included more often in group activities, they can be given more freedom of movement, they can be provided more choices of activities, they can increase their attention to learning new skills, and they will likely be less stressed and more happy.

The key principle in teaching young children to use self-control and withhold undesirable behaviors is to use positive reinforcement. As the undesirable behaviors occur less frequently or disappear completely, the child gets something he or she wants, such as attention, praise, smiles, a fun activity, or a special treat. Using positive reinforcement to increase self-control can be accomplished in a few simple steps.

Target a specific behavior to reduce or eliminate.

When a young child's misbehavior is serious, it is usually easy to identify specific behaviors to reduce, either in frequency or severity, or to eliminate. Although it may be difficult to do so, try to limit your target to just one behavior. Young children with autism/PDD will not understand if you focus on too many behaviors at once or you have too many requirements. The target behavior could be the one that is most dangerous, most harmful, or most disruptive, or the one that causes the most interference with learning and daily success. Prioritize and focus on just one behavior. Describe the behavior by using an action verb (see Chapter 7 for more information on target behaviors) so that everyone is clear about what the child should not do. For example, a goal for Rusty is to stop hitting.

Explain the behavior using visuals and modeling.

It helps to be simple, clear, and specific with young children. To explain what it is you don't want them to do, take a picture of the behavior, use an icon that represents it, or model the behavior directly. As you model and explain, be brief. Offering young children with autism/PDD long-winded explanations of why they shouldn't be doing something is usually pointless and ineffective. A simple phrase like, "No hitting," said clearly and while making direct eye contact, should be sufficient. You will also want to use visual supports and cues to communicate that the targeted behavior is something that you don't want to see. You can do this in several ways, including:

- Placing the universal "no" sign (red circle with a slash through it) over the picture of the behavior

- Putting an "X" on the visual

- Saying, "no" or "stop" firmly when the behavior occurs

- Using the American Sign Language sign for "no" or "stop" along with the verbal direction

Decide on the positive reinforcement and its use.

In the previous chapter on individual-trial teaching, we provided an extensive list of positive reinforcers that are preferred and appropriate for young children with autism/PDD. After selecting positive reinforcement that is likely to be effective, decide how often you will reinforce and what format will be used to deliver the reinforcement. Several formats and schedules work well, and these techniques can be used to reinforce self-control and the withholding of problematic behaviors and, of course, to reinforce desired, socially appropriate behaviors.

Puzzle Reinforcers

One of the most effective and engaging tools for positive reinforcement with young children who have autism/PDD is puzzles. Puzzles are quite simple to make and to use.

① First, take or find a picture of the activity or object that the child wants and that you are going to provide if he or she demonstrates self-control. With young children, it is often best to use a photograph of the actual object or activity. We recommend at least a 6" × 6" to 12" × 12" size so that it is clearly visible from a few feet away. If possible, laminate the picture or photo so that it is durable.

② Next, cut a puzzle board the same size as the picture and laminate this as well.

③ Cut the picture into pieces, creating a puzzle.

④ Trace the puzzle pieces onto the board, so that the outline of the puzzle pieces can be seen.

⑤ Attach Velcro to the back of each puzzle piece and its corresponding space on the puzzle board.

Before cutting the puzzle pieces, you will have to decide how many pieces to create. We recommend making two or three prints of the same picture, cutting the first one into only a few big pieces (two to four), cutting the second picture into smaller pieces (five to eight), and cutting the last puzzle into even smaller pieces (10 to 12). The child receives one piece of the puzzle after each successful time period of withholding the behavior. With a varying number of pieces, you can easily change your reinforcement criteria, requiring the child to withhold the behavior during just two or three time periods or as many as 12 time periods. The length of the time periods will vary, too, depending on the individual needs

of the child. For example, we have created a behavior puzzle for Lilly, who loves to turn the pages of a plastic book with a variety of textures. The puzzle has five pieces. Lilly's teacher gives her a piece after each 5-minute time period that she does not grab or pinch another student in the preschool class. After 25 minutes, Lilly could earn 5 minutes to sit and play with her plastic book. Caleb's teacher uses a three-piece puzzle with him. His goal is to stop walking away, and his puzzle is a picture of the sandbox. Not only are Caleb's time periods for self-control shorter than

Lilly's (2 minutes), he needs fewer pieces to complete his puzzle. In only 6 minutes, Caleb can earn time in the sandbox if he does not walk away from his teacher or the instructional assistant.

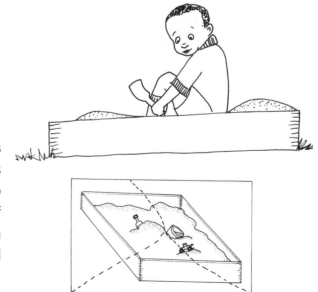

Charts and Other Visuals

There are many ways to visually represent progress for young children with autism/PDD. Simple charts, tracking forms, pictures, dot-to-dots, sticker books, stamp forms, and other visuals can all be used effectively to help young children learn to withhold undesired behaviors. These charts and other visuals should be part of the reinforcement system itself, not just representations of progress. For example, Lilly's team worked to help Lilly's parents teach her to stop throwing her food on the floor at mealtime. To reinforce her for "no mess," the team used a small card with several sections. They laminated the card and in the top section placed a picture of the family breakfast table with the chair Lilly sits in and the placemat that she uses. The photo showed no spilled or dropped food. In each of the three sections below the picture (for breakfast, lunch, and dinner), Lilly could earn a sticker of her favorite cartoon character if she kept her food on the table at each meal. When the card was full, Lilly could watch a cartoon after dinner, which was perfect for her parents, who were cleaning up after dinner at that time.

At the end of this chapter, we have provided several examples of visual contracts to help you as you improve the behavior of young children with autism/PDD. To use these positive reinforcement tools, set a goal with the child; then, after each occurrence of the target behavior, punch with a hole punch, color in with a marker, cover the holes with small stickers, or make a line. These can be used to increase or strengthen almost any behavior you are teaching.

Two-Step Visual

For young children with autism/PDD to understand the connection between a behavior and its consequence, there is almost no better tool than a two-step visual, which is a simple card that shows the desired behavior first and a positive reinforcer second. This is helpful in three important ways: it communicates the behavior and the consequence; it is a teaching tool that adults can use consistently in almost any environment; and it serves as a symbol of the positive reinforcement the child will earn after positive behavior. In Chapter 4, we discussed a two-step tool called First/Then. First, decide on the behavior you want the child to stop (No throwing) and then decide on the positive reinforcement—what the consequence will be if the child stops the behavior (Bubbles).

Use of the card should follow the same basic behavioral principles introduced in earlier chapters:

- Show the visual of the behavior.
- Tell the child what to do or not do.
- Model the behavior or absence of it.
- Show the visual of the positive reinforcer, along with the actual object if it is available.
- As soon as the child demonstrates the behavior (remember, the behavior might be the withholding of a behavior).
- Show the card again.
- Get excited, praise the child.
- Provide the positive reinforcer.

During this process, remember to use simple one- or two-word phrases that describe the behavior and the consequence. At first, the two-step contract should be used in short intervals, perhaps even 30 seconds or less. When teaching a child to stop screaming, even 15 seconds of no screaming will be welcome and should be reinforced.

At the end of this chapter, we have provided a simple two-part form that is one of the best tools for teaching behavior to young children. It can be used both to teach positive behaviors that adults would like to see demonstrated as well as to teach the high-level, difficult-to-learn, possibly most important behavior of all: self-control. In the next section of this chapter, we will provide suggestions for teaching positive behaviors (the behaviors you do want) that can replace the withheld behaviors (the behavior you don't want).

Positive Replacement Behaviors

The suggestions provided for teaching young children to use self-control and withhold undesirable or challenging behaviors can also be applied to teaching positive replacement behaviors. Most parents and professionals can easily transfer and use the same principles and ideas to teach new behaviors and skills. However, we have some additional strategies that should make this process easier and more effective.

Establish behavioral contingencies.

The first strategy is to establish contingencies. When events are contingent, one event is liable to happen because another event has happened. In behavioral terms, we know that because one thing happens (a positive consequence presented to the child), another thing is very likely to happen (the child demonstrates a desired behavior). Establishing contingencies is necessary for many young children with autism/PDD, who will not naturally imitate or demonstrate positive, desired behaviors.

One of the easiest ways to explain the process of establishing contingencies to teach a replacement behavior is to use an example. Caleb's father became concerned because when he and Caleb arrived at school in the morning and started to walk into the building, Caleb would break away and run. One day, Caleb nar-

rowly escaped being hit by a bus on the school driveway. His father wants Caleb to hold his hand and stay with him when they walk from the car into school. To do so, Caleb's father began to establish a simple two-part contingency: (1) Caleb had to hold his father's hand as they walked together from the car to the school. (2) If Caleb held his father's hand and stayed with him, Caleb received one of his favorite toys, a cube-shaped puzzle, to play with for 10 minutes. If Caleb did not stay with his father, he did not get the cube. Caleb's father wants him to learn the contingency: One event (playing with the cube) is more likely to occur if another event (holding Dad's hand) occurs.

To make sure that he has Caleb's attention and to increase Caleb's understanding, Caleb's father puts the cube on the dashboard of the car while they drive to school and then carries it in plain sight while they walk from the car to the building. Using the cube as a visual cue is important because Caleb sometimes has trouble remembering exactly what he is supposed to do.

When Caleb's father first started this routine, Caleb had a difficult time. He tried to break free, he cried, he screamed, and he resisted in every way he knew. To make progress, Caleb's father kept him moving. They didn't run into the school, but they did move quickly. This was a great idea because the less time there was available for resistance, the easier it was to get Caleb from the car into the school without a major tantrum. Caleb's father also held his son's hand firmly. He wasn't too tough but he helped Caleb understand what was expected. Once they were inside the school, if Caleb had held his hand and stayed with him, his father immediately gave him the cube. This was an important part of the plan. Caleb is a child for whom positive consequences should happen immediately if they are going to be effective. When Caleb refused to hold his father's hand  and did not get to play with cube, Caleb tantrummed several times. But Caleb's father stuck with his plan. After 2 weeks, the running away eventually became less and less of a problem. A month after the routine was started, Caleb had completely stopped running away from his father in the morning. Caleb learned an important new behavior and his father was able to relax knowing that Caleb was less likely to get hurt.

Use a timer to improve behavior.

In earlier chapters, we described the value of timers in teaching. Another example can help parents and professionals understand how to use this tool. Lilly has made good progress lately as she learns to attend to a task in her preschool classroom. However, her teacher knows that when Lilly goes into the general education class next year, she will be expected to do even better. To ensure Lilly's success, her teacher has begun to use a timer to carefully structure and increase the amount of time Lilly attends to an assigned activity. Lilly's teacher started the process by getting a baseline. For 2 weeks, she used a stopwatch around her neck and timed Lilly as she stayed engaged in activities in several different centers. After recording Lilly's on-task time for 2 weeks, the teacher computed an average for each of the areas and recorded it on a graph.

Next, the teacher began her intervention. In this case, the intervention was simple: When Lilly began to leave an area early, her teacher signaled her back and turned the timer to 2 minutes. If Lilly returned to her assigned area and remained for at least 2 additional minutes, until the timer sounded, her teacher enthusiastically praised her for "staying put" and put a plastic star on a magnet strip on Lilly's table. When the strip was filled with four stars, Lilly got to do one of her favorite activities: play a computer game that has her favorite song in it. After Lilly had 5 minutes at the computer, Lilly's teacher asked her to get back to her regular activities. Lilly quickly learned that if she would stay in her area and remain focused on the assignment, she would get to do something she liked. Lilly's movement around the room decreased and her attention to tasks increased. The teacher's graph, which she maintained for 2 months, was a good source of information for the professional team as well as Lilly's parents.

There are many behaviors required of young children when they enter a general education situation and success in some of them can be measured by the duration of the behavior. Using a timer as part of a simple, straightforward plan is often essential for improving children's behaviors in skills such as sitting, attending, making eye contact, and remaining in an assigned area. In Appendix 7 we provided a form (Duration Chart) that can be used to record the duration of behaviors.

Use data as the basis for behavioral planning.

In earlier chapters we stressed the importance of recording, graphing, and reviewing the occurrence of specific behaviors. We will not add a lengthy discussion to this prior information. However, we do want to demonstrate with another example how effective data collection, graphing, and review can be. Our example concerns Rusty, who as you already know, is an active, exuberant child. While everyone enjoys his energy and lively temperament, Rusty often does not complete what he is asked to do, even when he is capable of doing so. Rusty's mother wants him to "finish." Some of the tasks he should complete but does not include picking up his toys, hanging up his clothes, and taking his cup and plate to the sink. Rusty's teacher would also like him to finish tasks such as coloring his paper, building the block structure according the pattern, and putting together a puzzle. Rusty's team decided that "finishing" would be the next important behavior goal for him.

To improve this behavior, Rusty's mother and teacher first recorded how many "finish" requests they make and how many he completes each day for a week. They used this information to compute a percentage of tasks completed. Because this percentage was so low (only 25%), they immediately began to use positive reinforcement with Rusty. Each time he finished a job, they praised him, saying, "Good job, Rusty. You finished." Then they immediately used a hole punch and punched his rabbit card (a simple card with a picture of a rabbit and dots encircling the rabbit picture). This was important because Rusty's favorite activity is to feed the class pet rabbit. Rusty was told that when the punches completely circled the rabbit, he could not only feed the class rabbit, but pet it too. The card traveled back and forth from home to school. Mom and the teacher also continued to tally how many activities had been requested and how many tasks were completed. They computed his finish percentage

each day. Fortunately, Rusty learned quickly that he would get to feed and pet the rabbit more quickly if he completed what he was asked to do. His percentage of task completion shot up dramatically. At the 6-week review meeting, Rusty's mother and teacher reviewed the graph and determined that for the previous 2 weeks, Rusty had finished 85% of his assignments each day. They declared the plan a success. When Rusty is ready to move on to his next teacher and class, his team will have the records to share, which will help both Rusty and his new teacher get off to a great start. The graph paints a dramatic picture of what works with Rusty and how well he can do under the right circumstances. At the end of the chapter we have two graphs, one for recording frequencies and one for recording percentages. Both are simple and easy to use.

Know the child.

Our final suggestion for teaching and supporting good behavior is one that should guide all of us in all of our work with young children who have autism/PDD, whether the goal is to teach using play, structure the environment, teach using individual trials, or teach and support positive behaviors: Get to know the child. Regardless of the goal, focus on your individual child and his or her needs. We believe that using the strategies described in this book will improve the quality of instruction for our young children with autism/PDD. We hope that you find them as useful as we have designed them to be.

Supporting References and Resources

Carr, E. G., Dunlap, G., Horner, R. H., Koegel, R. L., Turnbull, A. P., Sailor, W., et al. (2002). Positive behavior support: Evolution of an applied science. *Journal of Positive Behavior Interventions, 4*(1), 4–16, 20.

Dettmer, S., Simpson, R. L., Myles, B. S., & Ganz, J. B. (2000). The use of visual supports to facilitate transitions of students with autism. *Focus on Autism and Other Developmental Disabilities, 15*(3), 163–169.

Gilmour, J., Hill, B., Place, M., Skuse, D. H. (2004). Social communication deficits in conduct disorder: A clinical and community survey. *Journal of Child Psychology & Psychiatry & Allied Disciplines, 45*(5), 967–979.

Hagopian, L. P., Wilson, D. M., & Wilder, D. A. (2001). Assessment and treatment of problem behavior maintained by escape from attention and access to tangible items. *Journal of Applied Behavior Analysis, 34*(2), 229–232.

Mueller, M. M., Wilczynski, S. M., & Moore, J. W. (2001). Antecedent manipulations in a tangible condition: Effects on stimulus preference on aggression. *Journal of Applied Behavior Analysis, 34*(2), 237–240.

Rogers, S. J. (2000). Interventions that facilitate socialization in children with autism. *Journal of Autism and Developmental Disorders, 30*(5), 399–409.

Wimpory, D. C., Hobson, R. P., Williams, J. M. G., & Nash, S. (2000). Are infants with autism socially engaged? A study of recent retrospective parental reports. *Journal of Autism and Developmental Disorders, 30*(6), 525–536.

Reproducible Forms

The forms on pages 160 through 167 can be used to record and reinforce children each time they demonstrate a target behavior. Set a goal with the child, then punch with a hole punch, color in with a marker, cover the holes with small stickers, or make a line after each occurrence of the target behavior.

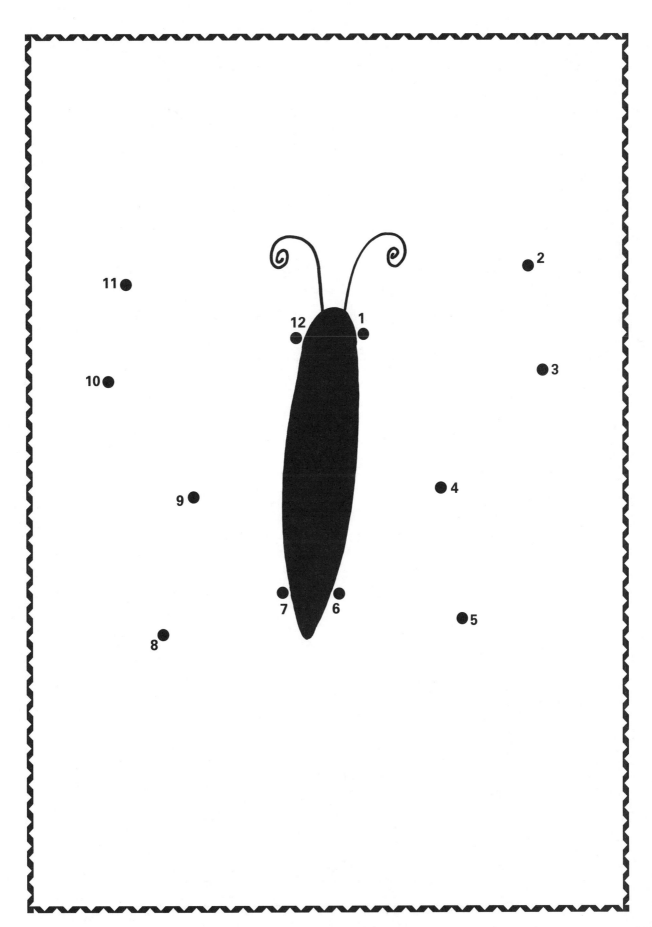

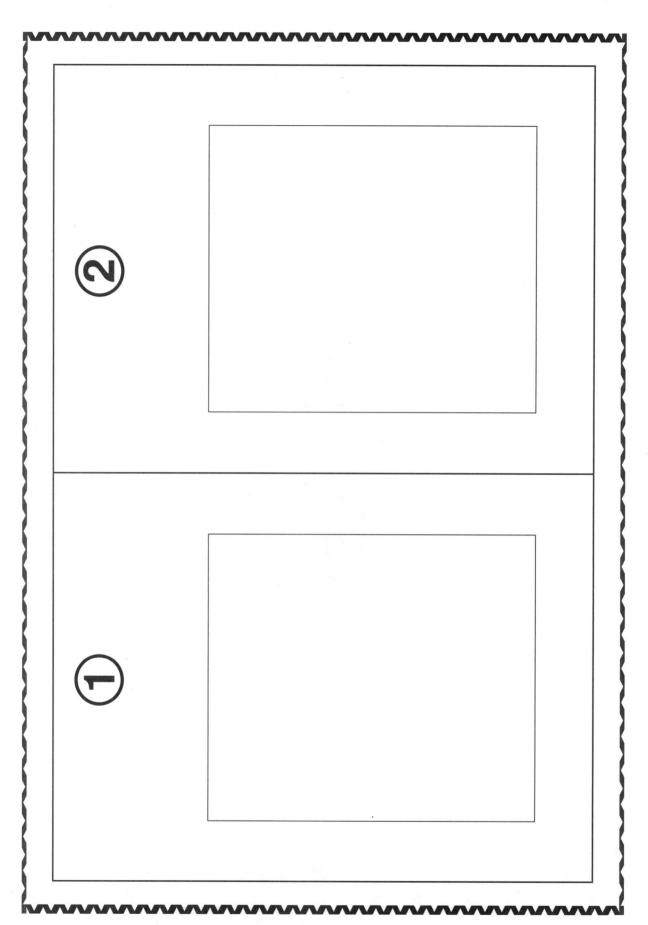

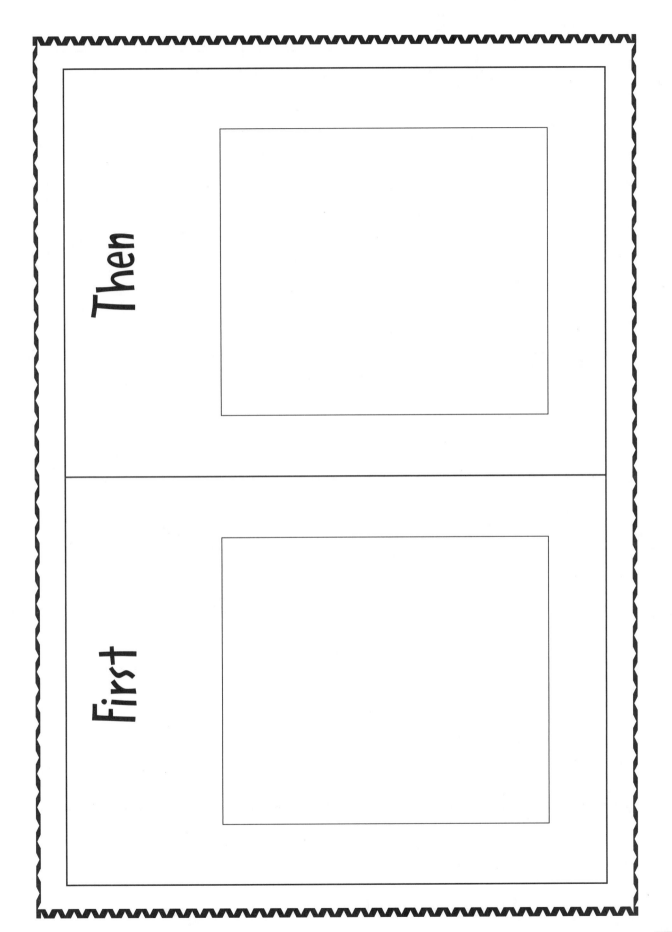

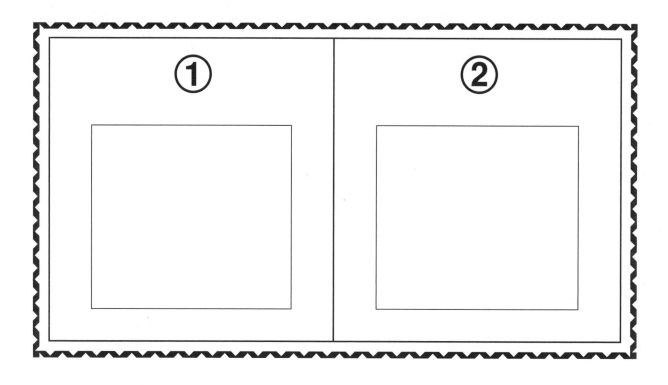

Frequency Chart

Student's Name _____

Behavior Being Tracked _____

Circle or mark through a number each time the behavior occurs. Begin with the number 1.

DATE									
F	10	10	10	10	10	10	10	10	10
R	9	9	9	9	9	9	9	9	9
E	8	8	8	8	8	8	8	8	8
Q	7	7	7	7	7	7	7	7	7
U	6	6	6	6	6	6	6	6	6
E	5	5	5	5	5	5	5	5	5
N	4	4	4	4	4	4	4	4	4
C	3	3	3	3	3	3	3	3	3
Y	2	2	2	2	2	2	2	2	2
	1	1	1	1	1	1	1	1	1
TIME	AM	PM	AM	PM	AM	PM	AM	PM	AM	PM

Percentage Chart

Name _____ Behavior _____

Record percentages of correct or completed activities and dates or times.

100%					
90%					
80%					
70%					
60%					
50%					
40%					
30%					
20%					
10%					
0					